A Family Raised on Sunshine

A Family Raised on Sunshine

by
Beverly K. Nye

Writer's Digest Books
9933 Alliance Road, Cincinnati, Ohio 45242

Designed by Robert Joseph Anzivino

Seventh Printing, December, 1978

Dedicated to

My patient and loving husband, Roy, and my four children, Stephen, Mark, Kristen and Heidi, who have filled our kitchen with sunshine for 22 years.

ACKNOWLEDGEMENTS

The sunshine that we share in our home has come from so many sources. First of course, from the willingness and co-operation of my special family. Roy has encouraged me in every experiment and opportunity I've had. The boys have always helped and supported me in every endeavor from our Bakery Route to eating up the leftovers! Kristen's sweet spirit and patience has kept me going and I especially am grateful for her skilled typing in preparing this manuscript. Heidi's desire to learn the homemaking skills and her love of cooking has kept me on my toes.

Many of the principles I've shared with you in this book, I owe to my mother, Gladys Boldt. Her confidence in me and the patience she has always shown makes her very special to me.

I would also like to thank my two terrific sisters, Maxine Haws and Donna Haack. So many ideas I use have come from them.

Thanks, too, to Elaine Cannon for encouraging me to put my ideas in book form.

Then, to my special friend, Marge Reeve. She has given me inspiration and encouragement when I needed it most and is a beautiful example of the type of person I would like to be.

I would also like to thank the many, many friends who have participated in my classes and in many ways have shared their ideas and love.

Finally, I would like to thank my Heavenly Father for the help and blessings he has given me. My enthusiasm for life comes from Him.

CONTENTS

Chapter I

Making Menus and Meals Memorable

Won't you come into my kitchen and visit with me a while? We are so blessed to be given the opportunity to be wives, mothers, and homemakers. I can't think of a more exciting challenge to awaken to each morning. You know, so much of our influence, teaching, loving, and caring takes place in our sunshiny kitchens. Many hours of family council, private chats, sharing of confidences, and laughing and learning together take place around the kitchen table. They say "the hand that rocks the cradle rules the world." Why not "the hand that kneads the bread shapes the family"? Many women today feel overwhelmed by the many facts and figures quoted to us daily and the rising cost of living and inflation. I would like to share with you some happy approaches to these problems and show you the way to have fun while saving money and feeding your family well.

Of course, as in everything else, a positive attitude is the first requirement. With a smile on our face and a song in our heart, we can lick any battle. Once you develop a desire to have a happy time improving your family's health, the first thing to do is to determine why you go grocery shopping. Our main purpose in buying food is to nourish our families. We know our bodies are the temples of our spirits, and it's our responsibility to give them proper care and respect by eating wisely. This should be our motivation.

We've all heard the old rules of thumb to never shop when you're hungry, rushed, or with children or husbands. Believe me, it *does* make a difference, so do try to plan your shopping trips accordingly. Also, make a list. This not only helps you to get the bargains of the week but also helps you to plan ahead. If there's an activity coming up, you'll be supplied, saving that extra trip to the store, and if there are especially busy days ahead, you can plan to serve something that's quick to fix.

Be sure you keep in mind balance and color in planning your meals, and make sure your family is getting the basic requirements:

> Grains and cereals
> Meats, eggs, and beans
> Milk, cheeses, and ice cream
> Fruits and vegetables

My mother taught me as a child that if the plate was attractive with a variety of colors in the foods, we could be pretty sure our meal was balanced. That makes meal planning a little more fun, too, and lets us exercise our artistic abilities. Texture plays another important part. Don't be afraid to expose your family to new foods. It makes mealtime exciting. Just be sure your positive and cheerful attitude is always showing. Who can refuse a confident, happy mother?

As our children were growing up, we enjoyed the experience of a new vegetable every Family Night. We've had many funny happenings and cherished family memories from this tradition. Our favorite memory was the evening we had parsnips. Our oldest son, Steve, was about four years old at the time and was a little hesitant about trying those "pale carrots". With hearty encouragement and a delicious mouthful, Daddy responded, "They're really good, Steve. Why, they put hair on your chest," as he spread his collar exposing his chest. Steve's eyes got as big as saucers, and we chuckled as during the rest of the meal, with every bite of parsnips, he peeked down his shirt! By the way, he still loves parsnips. New foods can be introduced to your family in many ways!

For our children's first experience with Oriental food we ate on the floor. There happened to be a tornado warning at the time (we were living in Kansas City) so it was even the basement floor, which added to the excitement. Needless to say, the children have fun thoughts of this type of food, and they're not particularly afraid of tornados because we were together enjoying life during these times, too.

Sometimes it's fun to dress up in costumes or share a souvenir if the new dish you are trying is of another locality or country. How about having a family member tell about the area the food is from? And it's always fun to enjoy a favorite recipe of a relative or special loved one and exchange anecdotes about the person during the meal.

Mealtime should always be pleasant, and I feel we have as big an obligation to see that what goes into our families' minds and hearts at this time is as pleasant, satisfying, and nourishing as the food we feed them. Include your family in your meal planning. Consider their needs and preferences. Try to have at least one thing everyone will enjoy.

Menus can be a fun thing for children. A menu exposes them to balanced meals, and the children become a part of the planning. With their artistic abilities, you can come up with some real cute conversation pieces at the table.

A favorite idea of mine came from an old Relief Society Magazine. Arising a few minutes earlier than usual, I fixed a pretty table complete with a small spring bouquet, baked a warm apple coffee cake, fixed juice, milk, and sausage, and then on each setting, I placed a cheery little menu listing the breakfast and said "Have a special, happy day." It was amazing the pleasant words that were spoken and good deeds done around our home that day.

Even a centerpiece can contribute to a pleasant meal. This can be anything from a special family treasure, a child's find of the day, a potted plant, or those dandelions little Mary picked after school. Be a little adventurous sometimes and change protocol. Take your plates and eat out under the tree in the yard. Even a winter picnic in the snow or a "pretend picnic" on the family room floor builds happy memories. Candlelight meals are always special, and it's surprising what an event a 25¢ candle can make of a meal.

One thing that we have felt strongly about in our home is that children learn proper etiquette and table manners. It has always been a custom that our Sunday dinner is served in the dining room with our good china, crystal, etc. This has helped the children feel comfortable with such things, and we never worry when they are eating away from home. Good manners make people feel so much more at ease and able to enjoy their surroundings. This was brought home to me by a story Elaine Cannon told about President Lee. Because his mother had taught him all the proper things about manners and protocol while dining as a child, President Lee was most comfortable while having dinner in the company of some very prominent foreign officials and was able to promote missionary work in these countries. This is but one example stressing how important it is that we teach our children to properly set a table, use a napkin, and sit gracefully.

A little hint that I didn't know until recently — as soon as you are finished with your food at the table, if you will lay your knife and fork together crosswise on your plate, it is a signal for the hostess or waiter to remove your plate. This rule of etiquette is internationally understood. Isn't it fun to learn new ideas?

Shopping and meal planning is certainly a challenge but it's so rewarding and exciting when you see those happy smiles on your family's faces.

CHEERFUL MORNING APPLE COFFEE CAKE

Dough

Mix together:

2/3 cup sugar
1/4 cup margarine
1 egg

Stir in:

1/2 cup milk

Then add:

1-1/2 cups flour
2 tsp. baking powder
1/2 tsp. salt

Streusel mixture

Mix together:

1/2 cup packed brown sugar
2 T. flour
2 T. melted butter
2 tsp. cinnamon
chopped nuts
1/2 tsp. nutmeg

Mix well and spread half of dough in 9x9 inch pan. Cover with apple slices and streusel mixture, top with other half of dough, and bake at 375° for 25-35 minutes.

Chapter II
Ways to Save with Fruits and Vegetables

Now that we've discussed some ideas on basic meal planning, let's spend some time on an imaginary trip to the grocery store. I'd like to share some interesting ideas and facts with you.

Let's start with the fruit and vegetable counters. These often neglected foods are one of the most important in our diet. In order to be successful here, we need to know how to buy, how to keep, and how to prepare them.

In buying any fruits or vegetables, always remember that fresh is best, then frozen, and then canned. Many things keep better if they are not washed immediately, especially berries. Always be careful when you do wash fruits and vegetables that you don't allow them to soak in water for a long time. Many nutrients can be lost through soaking. Also remember not to peel any vegetable or fruit if it isn't necessary. All those good vitamins lie right beneath the skin so please don't cut them away.

I always clean my celery, radishes, and a few carrots, and some cauliflower as soon as I return home from shopping. This way when a snack is desired, there are vegetables handy. Just keep each vegetable in a plastic bag and see how much everyone will enjoy them. If your family needs a little more protein, a cheese spread, dip or peanut butter goes great with them.

As you cook fresh or frozen fruits or vegetables, always use as little water as possible and don't boil the life out of them. Most things taste better if they are a little undercooked and are better for you, too. This brings up a favorite little trick I'd like you to try. Always keep several mason jars in the freezer section of your frige. Into one, pour all the leftover juices you have from any vegetables. This will make a great stock to add to gravies, stews, or soups. Into another, drop all the leftover vegetables from your meals. Even that one carrot slice or two peas. As these leftovers accumulate, they sure come in handy for vegetable soups, meat pies, or casseroles. Why pay for expensive mixed vegetables when we can make our own combinations every day of the week? Into a third jar, pour all your leftover fruit juices. These juices are very good used as a fruit sauce or in jellos, puddings, or fruit drinks.

When you're shopping, be sure you keep in mind the reasons you are purchasing these fruits or vegetables. If you plan to make applesauce, of course you wouldn't buy the choicest apples for 15¢ apiece. When you have that last overripe banana on the counter that no one will eat, mash it up with a fork and freeze it in a container until you want to make some nut bread or cookies. Oftentimes you can pick up ripe bananas at the store for a considerable savings and do the same thing. Just package the mashed bananas in quantities the size your recipe calls for.

11

Here's my favorite:

BANANA NUT BREAD

Cream:

½ cup shortening
1-1/3 cups sugar

Add:

2 large bananas (sliced)
2 T. milk

Mix well with mixer, add:

2 eggs, and blend.

Mix together and add:

1-3/4 cups flour
1/2 tsp. soda
1-1/2 tsp. baking powder
1 tsp. salt
1 tsp. nutmeg

Fold in 1 cup chopped nuts. Bake at 350° for 30 minutes, then 325° for 15-20 minutes or until done.

Notice that touch of nutmeg in the recipe. Sure makes it good! Nutmeg is also a great addition sprinkled over parsnips or rhubarb sauce. Try it!

When buying fruits and vegetables (or meats for that matter) in bags or packages or things such as celery, always weigh them. You know, by government standards weights are allowed to vary some, and you might as well be getting your money's worth.

Always buy things in season and when they are most plentiful. In most areas, you can go to your local wholesale produce buyers and buy things by the crate or case. One of our favorite "bulk purchases" is grapefruit. For Family Home Evening, we assemble around the table; then one family member cuts the grapefruits in half, the next cuts around the sections, the next scoops the sections into a clean jar, and the last squeezes in their juice. Nothing else needs to be added. Just stick your jar into the freezer (be sure you leave a little expansion space in the top of the jar), then when grapefruit is out of season, you can just whip out a jar and serve it with maybe a cherry added on top — fresh tasting and delicious! Knowing you saved a lot, too!

This is also fun to do with melons. Our favorite is cantaloupe balls (or small chunks) covered with orange juice or 7-UP. Melon balls covered with orange juice are a great beginning for a cold winter morning. The ones covered with 7-UP make a delicious and impressive appetizer before an evening meal. (It also lets you feel a little smug and proud serving cantaloupe in the wintertime at such a low cost.) A mint leaf is pretty added to the appetizer. On the watermelon balls, I use a light sugar syrup (1 cup sugar to 3 cups water) cooled and poured over the melon balls. You can also use the syrup with a melon mixture or with grapes or some other type of fruit. This combination makes a pretty appetizer, also. Just be sure when freezing anything you allow a good inch of headspace in the jar for expansion and then serve when still a little icy.

Now that you've used up the inside of your watermelon, don't even throw away the rind. Please try this delicious watermelon rind pickle recipe.

WATERMELON PICKLES

Peel and remove all green and pink portions from the rind of one large watermelon. Cut in 1 inch cubes and soak overnight in salt water (4 T. salt to 1 qt. water). Drain, cover with fresh water, and cook until almost tender. Drain again.

Mix together:

4 cups sugar
2 cups vinegar
4 tsp. whole cloves
8 sticks cinnamon
A little mustard seed

Tie spices in cheesecloth bag. Heat the syrup and spices to boiling and allow to set for 15 minutes. Add drained watermelon rind and cook until clear and transparent. Pack at once into jars and seal.

If your family likes the Royal Anne or Bing cherries canned, and you are not fortunate enough to live where they are plentiful, try another little fun idea:

MOCK CHERRIES

Wash and stem seedless green grapes. Pack into jars. Fill jars to within 1/2 inch of top with light sugar syrup. Add 1 T. cherry concentrate and red food coloring to desired color.

Process according to time-table for grapes.

It's amazing what a little variety can do! Sometimes when I can pears, I add a little green food coloring and a touch of mint extract to a few bottles. These are so good in the winter, served on a lettuce leaf with a scoop of cottage cheese and cherry on top.

One of the most popular vegetables is the potato, so let's talk about potatoes for a minute. I suppose it's a matter of personal preference, but I like to use the whites for baking and the reds for boiling. Remember how we talked about not peeling our fruits and vegetables? Since we are concerned with both saving and nutrition, try this: Whenever you have just one thing to go in the oven, such as a cake, never waste all that surrounding oven space and heat. Scrub and wrap in foil all the potatoes that will fit into the leftover space and bake them, too. I always try to keep a supply of these baked potatoes in my vegetable crisper. They make terrific hash browns (don't even remove the skins). They are also much more flavorful in potato salad or any dish where you would usually use peeled and boiled potatoes. Try potato pancakes served with warm applesauce and sausage — yum yum! Delicious! If you should ever peel potatoes, remember to peel them *thinly* and then don't throw away the water. It's a great addition to breads and yeast doughs. However, do refrigerate it if you aren't ready to use it right away.

Thank goodness for the blender when it comes to cole slaw. My family loves it, and what a job it used to be. Now I just put about 3 cups of water in the blender, add some cut up cabbage, and Zip! Cole slaw in a minute or two. Don't make juice, though. That's easy to do. It only takes a few flips of the switch. When I drain the cabbage, I use the juice to cook a vegetable in or steam some frankfurters or Kielbasa sausage. Once you've made your cole slaw, it's also delicious to vary it with peanuts, apples, pineapple, bananas, etc.

Winter squash is usually quite plentiful and reasonably priced in most areas. At that time of year, I fill my oven with whole Butternut or pieces of Hubbard or Banana squash and bake them all at once. Then I scoop out the squash and pack it in meal size bags and freeze. When I'm ready to serve it, then all I have to do is lay the frozen squash on a pie plate and bake it. It is so fast and easy. Remember, too, to save the seeds as you cut open the big squash. Dry them to plant next year. Pumpkin can also be cooked and frozen in this way. The seeds are good roasted and seasoned.

As you add new types of vegetables to your family's meals also vary the way in which you serve the standard kinds. Here are two good recipes that also use up other leftovers, like bread and rice.

CARROT CASSEROLE

Cook:

12 carrots (sliced)

Make sauce of:

1 chopped onion
1/4 cup margarine
1/4 cup flour
1 tsp. salt
1-1/4 tsp. dry mustard
2 cups milk
Dash of pepper
Dash of celery salt

3 cups buttered bread crumbs
1/2 lb. grated sharp cheese

Arrange layers of carrots, cheese, and crumbs (twice). Pour sauce over and sprinkle with crumbs. Bake at 350° for 45 minutes.

COUNTRY RICE

Mix together in 2-qt. casserole:

3 cups cooked rice
1/2 cup chopped parsley
1/2 cup grated cheddar cheese
1/2 cup chopped onion
2 T. chopped green pepper
1 clove garlic (minced)

Blend and mix into rice:

14-1/2 oz. can evaporated milk
2 eggs (beaten)
1/2 cup vegetable oil
1 T. salt
Dash of celery salt
1/2 tsp. pepper
3 T. lemon juice

Sprinkle with paprika. Bake at 350°
for 45 minutes or until set.

As you adopt some of the ideas in this chapter, I'm sure you'll find that you are having less and less waste. Before anything goes down the disposal or into the garbage, ask yourself if there is a use for it. Even apple peels make a delicious jelly, and there's a recipe in every pectin box. All the seeds you remove from fruits and vegetables make lovely plants —avocado seeds (and, by the way, you can mash and freeze avocado if you get a good deal at the market on ripe ones; just add a dash of lemon juice.), pineapple tops, orange and lemon seeds, even carrot tops in a lid of water produce a lacy little plant. You know, even if your plants die, they're not a fruitless investment!

Before we leave the subject of fruits and vegetables, let's talk a minute about juices and drinks.

Orange juice is probably the most popular juice purchased. You might like to know that all frozen orange juice concentrates have to measure up to the same government standards so whichever brand you prefer, feel comfortable buying it, regardless of price. However, do vary your fruit or juice in the morning. Orange juice isn't the only source of Vitamin C. Tomato juice is a good Vitamin C juice, also. I have a recipe using tomato juice that I enjoy serving my family or guests before dinner. Try it!

INGE MIDGLEY'S TOMATO JUICE COCKTAIL

Mix together:

1 large can tomato juice
1 tsp. grated onion
3 T. lemon juice or cider vinegar
1/4 tsp. celery salt
1-1/2 tsp. salt
1 T. Worcestershire sauce
1 tsp. horseradish
1 tsp. sugar
1/4 tsp. paprika
1/4 tsp. Tabasco sauce

Stir well. Chill.

When you purchase large cans of juices, you should be aware of the words used in labeling and how they are used according to government standards. If the label says "juice" as the final word, the can must contain 100% juice; if the last word is "drink", it must contain only 50% juice; and if it says "ade", it must contain only 25% juice. The word "punch" only requires 10% juice. That means that can contains an awful lot of water, sugar and additives. We can dilute our juices down ourselves to make cool drinks for our families for a lot less money, and they won't be getting all that sugar and coloring, either. Try to avoid all the sugar drinks and punches. They really waste our food dollar, and they're not good for our bodies, either. There are so many nutritious fruit juices to drink and you know, there's nothing like a good glass of water. After all, we need that every day, too, and water doesn't have to be sweetened! Our family especially enjoy a very easy grape juice we can in the summer. It's so good and nutritious as a drink and also terrific in the blender with a scoop of ice cream.

QUICK GRAPE JUICE

Wash 1 cup Concord grapes and pack into quart jar.

Add: 1/2 cup sugar and fill jar with boiling water.

Process in water bath for 30 minutes.

Heidi never can get enough of this. In fact, this is the first thing she always offers our guests.

"Orange Delicious" (an Orange Julius type of drink) is another family favorite. This recipe can also be made extra good for breakfast by adding an egg, wheat germ, honey, etc.

ORANGE DELICIOUS

1 can orange juice (frozen)
1-1/2 cups cold water
1/2 cup milk
1/2 cup sugar
1 tsp. vanilla
1 tray of ice cubes

Mix in blender, adding ice slowly.

Milk is one of the staples in the drink line. This can also be made more economical if mixed half and half with powdered milk. However, be sure you check prices because, oftentimes, depending on availability of milk, you can buy 2% milk just as reasonably as mixing it. Do use your powdered milk in cooking, though. I always keep a glass jar of powdered milk handy on my kitchen counter. A handful in meatloaf, meatballs, cookie dough, or pancake batter just adds extra nutrition if your family doesn't drink the milk they should.

On my counter, I also keep a large jar of cocoa mix. This is handy to have and fun to make in a hurry. It's the first cocoa mix I've come up with that doesn't look and taste like brown water! As well as serving it as a hot drink, it's great thrown into the blender with some cold water and a scoop of ice cream or some ice cubes.

COCOA MIX

Mix together in large mixing bowl:

13 cups powdered milk

1 lb. box instant hot chocolate powder (Nestles or Hershey's)

11 oz. instant cream powder (such as Cremora or Pream)

4 T. powdered sugar

When serving, put 1/4 cup powder in tea cup, fill with hot water, add marshmallows if desired.

Hardly a night passes without Mark's traditional cup of hot chocolate and his plate of cookies.

Here is a mix I've also made using Ovaltine.

OVALTINE MIX

Mix together in large mixing bowl:

2 T. powdered sugar

8 cups powdered milk

One 9 oz. jar Ovaltine

6 oz. instant cream powder (such as above)

When serving use in the same proportions as above.

Condensed milk is a type of milk we use often in cooking. I'd like to share a recipe of mine with you so you can make your own at a fraction of the cost.

MARILYN'S CONDENSED MILK

Stir until dissolved:

1 cup boiling water
1/2 cup butter
2 cups sugar
2 cups powdered milk

Beat until smooth — will be thin, but thickens later on. Can be done in blender. Makes 1 quart.

To really be saving at your house, when your jam jar is nearly empty and everyone avoids it like the plague, fill it with milk, and if you like, some crushed ice and have your little ones shake it with fervor. It makes a delicious fruit flavored drink and cleans the jar at the same time. The kids love it!

Pop is one of the biggest drains on the average food budget. The thing we must remember is that our food dollar is to nourish our bodies, and this applies to the things we drink as well as what we eat. Try buying pop out of recreation money instead of food money. That is really all it amounts to, anyway.

See how creative you can be with the wholesome fruits, vegetables, juices, and good milk that the Lord has given us, and watch how much better everyone feels.

Chapter III

Magic Money with Meats

Meat can be one of the biggest expenses we have in our food budget, so let's have fun saving money in this area. There are special times of the year when certain types of meat are most plentiful. At these times we should plan our grocery budget so we can stock up our freezers and take advantage of the additional saving. Watch for:

Beef in July and January
Lamb - September
Pork - November
Veal - May
Fryers - June thru August
Turkeys - October and November

As we think about different types of meat, let's discuss some of their uses. Beef seems to be the most popular, so let's begin with beef. There are so many different categories of ground beef to consider. I feel that the very inexpensive hamburger wastes so much in fat, water, and filler (which is usually added to the beef) that I like to buy the better grade. In fact, if sirloin patties are on special and comparable to ground beef in price, I always buy them. Two patties will make a nice batch of spaghetti, chili, or soup since there is no waste.

MY SPAGHETTI

Mix together:

1 lb. hamburger (browned)
1 onion (finely chopped)
4 T. bouillon powder
1/2 tsp. salt
pepper to taste
1 can tomato sauce
1 can tomato paste
2 cups hot water
2 tsp. sugar
1/2 tsp. basil
1/2 tsp. oregano
Dash of garlic

Simmer for one hour and serve over 1 lb. spaghetti.

This spaghetti recipe is adequate for 1 lb. spaghetti (about six average servings). It is also a tremendous sauce to use in Lasagna or other Italian dishes. I like to layer the sauce with slices of eggplant, dipped in flour and fried, then sprinkle mozzarella cheese over each layer. Bake at 375° for 30-35 minutes. It's delicious!

MOM'S OLD FASHIONED CHILI

Brown:

1 lb. hamburger
1 large onion (chopped)
1/2 green pepper (chopped)

Add:

2 cans tomato soup and water
1 qt. canned tomatoes
2 cans kidney beans
2 T. chili powder

Let simmer for 1 hour.

CLEVELAND CHILI

Brown:

3 lbs. hamburger
3 big onions (chopped)
5 garlic cloves (minced)

Add:

1 qt. rich stock
1 can tomato paste
3 T. chili powder
1 tsp. cumin
1 tsp. oregano
salt to taste
Tabasco sauce to taste

Let simmer for one hour.

Whenever you use a roast or similar cut of meat be sure you use the scraps and bone to cook up a good soup stock. Just brown all the trimmings in a little of the suet or fat rendered from the meat, then cover with 1 to 1-1/2 qts. water, add some onion seasonings, and simmer slowly for several hours. At this point, strain the broth and add what vegetable you like, and return the pieces of meat to the broth. Cook until vegetables are done, and you have a great soup. If you choose to save the broth, just store it in a jar in the refrigerator. It is wonderful for gravy, or thicken it and use it as a base for a meat pie. It's also great for chili.

Some people like to buy half a beef for their freezers, but our family has found it is much more feasible for us to watch the specials and stock up on a particular cut when it's most available. This way we avoid wasting cuts of meat we don't care for, and it spreads the cost out a little, too. The meat men are usually most accommodating and will do any cutting you ask them to. They also can be very helpful in advising you on the tenderness of a cut or whatever you'd like to know. Don't hesitate to take advantage of their knowledge.

Please don't waste your good food dollars on expensive and artificial tenderizers. There are many good basic foods you can use. Tomato juice, lemon juice, and vinegar to name a few. Then, if, for instance, you use tomato juice as a tenderizing marinade, use it in cooking your meat, too, because the marinade's full of good juices and vitamins from the meat. Don't pour it down the drain.

Also, ask your butcher for a piece of suet and keep it handy in your freezer. A small piece, browned in a pan is great for adding flavor to extra lean cuts of meat. Then in making gravy, broth, or soup from the drippings, if you feel you have too much grease or fat in it, simply take an ice cube and skim the top of the liquid. The fat will harden around the ice cube, and you can just throw it away. Another little trick to remember if you get too much salt in anything—add a chunk of raw potato, let it cook awhile, and the potato will absorb some of the salt.

Now, let's talk about pork for a little while. The prime thing to remember here is that pork always needs to be *well* done. Pork can carry the germ for Trichinosis and for this reason must be well cooked. In buying pork, it is usually more economical to buy larger cuts. Then when you get home, you can cut up your pork chops or divide a pork roast. One of the most favorite dishes in our home is the way we fix Pork and Sauerkraut.

PORK AND SAUERKRAUT

Brown well on all sides, one pork loin roast.

Add:

One large can sauerkraut with juice
2 heaping T. brown sugar
1 bay leaf

Cover tightly and simmer for 4-6 hours.

Another way we like pork is roasted with potatoes and gravy. For this meal, I brown the roast well (and this should always be done slowly so it is well browned on all sides with some good drippings in the bottom of the pan), salt and pepper it, and then lay several bay leaves on top. This gives an extra good flavor to the meat and also to the gravy. I always remember the delicious pork Mom would bottle on the farm as we butchered our hogs in the fall. A bay leaf went in every jar — yum! What a delicious aroma!

Although we all love the flavor of bacon, we shouldn't count on this as a serving of protein. It is merely enjoyed for flavor, because the nutritional benefit is very small. However, the flavor does wonders for things. There's nothing like a steaming tureen of my potato soup on a crisp, cool fall evening with a loaf of homemade bread and honey and a few crunchy carrot sticks and apple slices to go along.

POTATO SOUP

Cook together:

6 potatoes (diced)
1/2 cup onion (chopped)
2 stalks celery (chopped)
2 tsp. salt
1 tsp. celery salt
2/3 tsp. pepper

Cover all with water and cook until tender.

Fry 8 slices of bacon, save 6 T. drippings. Make white sauce of 6 T. drippings, 2 T. flour, and 2 cups milk.

Add white sauce to soup, crumble bacon and add. Heat thoroughly.

Sausage is a good source of protein for breakfast, but why only think of sausage as a breakfast meat? One of my greatest dollar stretchers is made with sausage.

TAMALE BALLS

Combine and mix well with hands:

1 lb. ground beef
1 lb. ground pork
1-1/2 cups corn meal
3/4 cup tomato juice
1/2 cup flour
4 garlic cloves (finely chopped)
1 T. chili powder
2 tsp. salt

Form into small balls. Place in following sauce and simmer for two hours.

Sauce:

5 cups tomato juice
1 T. chili powder
2 tsp. salt

Ham is, of course, the all time favorite. I prefer to watch for the sales on boneless ham and buy several. Then I have my butcher slice them in slices comparable to lunch meat. When I get home these slices are repackaged in meal-sized bags and frozen. Then I'm ready for scalloped potatos and ham, sandwiches, or any type of casserole we'd like. Occasionally, I buy the butt portion of a whole ham to bake. Then when nearly all the ham is used off the bone, I cover the bone with water, a couple of chopped onions, salt and pepper, and 1 lb. of great northern beans. After this has simmered about 3-4 hours and the beans are nearly cooked, I add several carrots sliced, and a good dash of catsup, brown sugar, and vinegar. Sure makes a delicious soup with some cornbread on the side.

While we're on the subject of pork, I'd like to share with you a family specialty recipe from my grandmother. As a child, I remember many cold winter Nebraska mornings with a steaming plate of Gritvous. My two boys can never get enough.

GRITVOUS

Cover 3-4 lbs. pork neck bones with water, add salt, and simmer for 3-4 hours.

Take meat out to cool and strain juice.

Add 2 lbs. steel cut oats to strained juice and cook for 3-4 hours more, stirring very often (low heat).

Before last hour of cooking, add meat picked from bones, 1 lb. raisins, 1 tsp. allspice, and 1 tsp. cinnamon.

Spoon into greased bread pans and freeze.

When ready to serve, slice and fry in hot fat.

Let's take some time now for chicken and turkey. I think the first thing I'd like to discuss with you is how to cut up chicken. Isn't it atrocious how they "butcher" a chicken in the stores? The first thing to do is cut off the wings. If you bend them back, the joint socket will automatically pop. Then, with the chicken on its side, cut off the thigh and leg. Then separate the leg from the thigh, again bending and popping the joint. Now cut the chicken all the way down the middle separating the breast from the back. Cut the back in two pieces. At this point you can either cut the breast in half lengthwise, or crosswise cut off the wishbone piece and cut the remaining piece in half, which is how we prefer it. This works best if your chicken is a little larger. It is so easy to cut up your own chicken and much more economical, too. Besides, you have the pieces as you like.

Instead of actually "frying" my chicken, I take a 9 x 13 glass pan and melt one stick of margarine in a 425° oven. While the butter is melting, I shake my chicken pieces in a paper bag of flour and seasonings (a little parmesan cheese is good). Then I lay them in the pan of butter, skin side down, and bake for a half hour, turn the pieces over and bake for a half hour more. The best crispy chicken you've ever tasted!

I always "fry" only the meaty pieces, and then I make a chicken stock with the back, wings, and neck. These I cover with water, salt and pepper, some onion and celery and simmer until the chicken is done. Strain your broth, add rice or noodles, cook until tender, and add the chicken meat picked from the bones. If you prefer, you may just refrigerate the strained broth and meat for later use in a casserole, etc.

Another great recipe for Sunday dinner after church is my chicken rice casserole. Make it in the morning and it's steamy hot and ready to eat by the time you get home!

CHICKEN RICE CASSEROLE

Place 1 cup uncooked rice in bottom of greased casserole. Lay pieces of 1 cut up fryer on rice. Sprinkle with 1 package dry onion soup.

Combine:

1 can chicken soup
2 cups milk
salt and pepper (use sparingly)

Pour over chicken.

Bake at 300° for 2-1/4 hours. Cover with foil for first part of baking time.

Turkeys can be a tremendous buy, and, of course you know, the bigger they are, the more meat you get per pound. The best and easiest way to prepare a turkey is in a brown paper bag. Simply prepare your turkey as usual, wash and dry it well, rub a small amount of salt inside the cavity, stuff as desired (never stuff ahead of time), and then rub an unsalted fat (solid shortening) all over the bird. If you use a fat with salt in it such as margarine, you'll get a hard crisp skin. Now slide the bird into a large brown grocery bag, fold the end of the bag over several times, fasten it securely with paper clips or staples, place the bag on a roaster or a pan with a rack, put it into a pre-heated (325°) oven, and cook for 20 minutes per pound if the bird's over 12 lbs. and 25 minutes per pound if it's under 12 lbs. The most important part is not to peek at all until the time is up. Then carefully tear the paper back, and you will have a beautifully browned and tender, juicy turkey with lots of drippings for delicious gravy. Remove the stuffing immediately and slice the turkey. I also keep several plastic bags of turkey in the freezer for later meals.

Don't forget about the miscellaneous meats, such as heart, tongue, and liver. They are great budget beaters. I like to fry a couple of slices of bacon until they are crisp and then cook my onion slices and floured liver slices in the drippings. It gives a great flavor. Be sure you don't overcook the liver. It cooks fast.

Fish is another "meat" that can be easy on the budget and also very good for us nutrition-wise. This is a great casserole served with crisp "Hush Puppies" (see Chapter 7).

LOIS'S WHITE FISH CASSEROLE

Boil Halibut or any large full fillets of white fish until meat is tender and falls from bones.

Make a cream cheese sauce:

2 T. margarine
2 T. flour
1/4 tsp. salt
1 cup milk
1 cup grated sharp cheese

Flake fish into sauce, place in a shallow casserole, and cover with bread crumbs.

Bake at 350° until brown and serve.

It seems like a good portion of our meat or protein dollar is spent on luncheon meats. I really feel that we don't get our dollar's worth here because of the many fillers and additives that they contain. We try to avoid them at our house; so let me share with you some of the many things we enjoy on our sandwiches.

First, I watch for a good buy on a nice roast. Many times roasts are more reasonable than luncheon meats. Then I roast the meat slowly so I don't get much shrinkage and it's nice and moist. (This can also be done in a paper bag like we do our turkey.) After I take the roast from the oven and cool it, I slice it into nice slices and immediately place the bags of slices into the freezer. By placing waxed paper between the slices you are ready for a sandwich at the drop of a hat. Meat loaf also makes a good sandwich. Whenever you only have one thing in the oven, utilize the heat by baking up several meat loaves, then slicing and freezing them for sandwiches. These can be seasoned in a variety of ways.

All of the canned fishes make delicious sandwiches and give you 100% good nutrition. We especially like chopped sweet pickle, walnuts, and celery in our tuna salad.

Don't forget about all that turkey that you can slice and freeze. When they are on special, you can make some real tasty sandwiches for lots less than luncheon meat. Remember also the boneless hams we had the butcher slice and then froze in meal-size bags. When chicken is especially reasonable, it's fun to fry up a big batch of chicken (in your oven, remember) and then freeze individual pieces in bags to be taken in a lunch. There's nothing like it with a piece of delicious homemade whole wheat bread and some fresh relish sticks.

Egg salad makes a satisfying and nutritious sandwich. As you are mixing up your chopped egg and mayonnaise, try adding a touch of mustard. It really gives the salad some zip!

Of course, there's always the traditional peanut butter. This is a great way to get protein. Try some spread on celery or a banana.

If your small children take their lunches in a lunch box with a thermos, a fun treat in the winter is to fix a thermos of hot tomato soup, tie a thread around a wiener and drop it in to the soup, leaving the end of the thread hanging out. Then fix a bun with the trimmings and at lunch time, PRESTO!, a hot dog and yummy flavored soup. Even husbands enjoy this on a cold day.

Chapter IV

More Magic Money with Meat Substitutes

There are many meat substitutes that we should try to include in our daily meals. They are extra good for us, more economical, and easy to store.

Beans are number one. There are so many varieties to choose from — try them all! When you are making the ham and beans soup I mentioned earlier, try the large or baby limas. It's a whole different taste treat. Split pea and lentil soup are also two of our favorites and are great to use up those scraps of ham.

This soup is easy to make and economical. We like cheese wedges, crispy french bread, and celery and apple slices with it.

LENTIL SOUP

Brown:
1/2 onion (chopped)
1 T. butter

Add:
2 qts. cold water
2 cups (1 lb. pkg.) dry lentils

Bring to a boil, cover and simmer for about 2 hours.

Add:
Several sliced carrots
1-2 celery stalks with leaves (chopped)
2-3 potatoes (grated)
1 tsp. basil
1 cup tomatoes
1 tsp. salt

Continue simmering with cover on until vegetables are tender. Serve with grated cheese on top if desired.

SPLIT PEA SOUP

Soak 2 cups dried split peas in 3 qts. cold water overnight.

Add:

1 ham bone with some meat left on it
1 large onion (minced)
3 stalks celery (chopped fine)
1 sprig parsley
bay leaf
1 cup carrots (sliced)

Heat to boil, cover and simmer 4-5 hours, until peas are tender and liquid is partially cooked down.

Season to taste with salt and pepper.

A few minutes before serving, add 1 cup cream. Stir in well and heat through.

Our family really enjoyed our two year stay in Texas because one of our first loves in food is Mexican. This is a good type of food to help the budget, too, because you can use lots of beans and corn meal. Corn meal is a good meat stretcher. I like to thicken my chili with it or use it in breading my meats. It gets so nice and crispy. Liver is good this way.

Here are some of our "family specials".

MEXICAN CHICKEN BAKE

Cube 2 lbs. cooked, boned chicken

Mix together:

1 can cream of mushroom soup
1/2 cup milk
1 small can green chilies
1 cup onion, chopped

Place one cup crushed Doritos in bottom of greased shallow casserole dish.

Next place half the chicken.

Cover it with half of soup mixture.

Repeat three layers again—1 more cup crushed Doritos and other halves of chicken and soup mixture.

Top with 1 cup grated cheddar cheese.

Bake at 300° for 40 minutes to one hour.

TEXAS GRITS

Boil together for 5 minutes:

6 cups boiling water
1-1/2 cups quick grits
1 tsp. salt

Add:

2 tsp. savory salt
1 stick margarine
1 lb Velveeta cheese (cut in chunks)
3 dashes Tabasco sauce
3 well-beaten eggs

Bake at 250° for one hour.

MEXI-CHILI CASSEROLE

Brown:

1 lb. hamburger

Add:

1 can kidney beans
1 can mild enchilada sauce
1 can tomato sauce
1 small onion (chopped)
1-1/2 cups cheese (grated)
6 oz. package corn chips (minus 1 cup)

Bake at 375° in 2 qt. casserole uncovered for 20-25 minutes. Spread the top with 1-1/2 cups sour cream. Sprinkle with 1/2 cup cheese (grated) and corn chips around edge. Return to oven for 3-4 minutes.

SOMBRERO DIP

Brown together:

1/2 lb. hamburger
1/4 cup onion (chopped)

Add:

1/4 cup catsup
1-1/2 tsp. chili powder
1/2 tsp. salt
1 can kidney beans (mashed)
dash of hot sauce

Heat thoroughly.

Garnish with:

1/2 cup grated cheese
1/4 cup onion
1/4 cup olives

Serve with tortilla chips.

HOT TACO SAUCE

Combine:

1 can (8 oz.) tomato sauce
1 T. vinegar
1 T. vegetable oil
1 clove garlic (pressed)
1/4 tsp. oregano
1 can (4 oz.) green chilies, chopped
1/2 tsp. hot pepper sauce

(This hot sauce is also delicious served as a dip with tortilla chips.)

As you know, cheese is a good source of protein, but there are several things we should know about it to get the most for our money. When the package lists moisture content, it's just a glorified way to say water, so be aware of that. Cottage cheese is the best source of protein, with American cheese being next in line.

Words on the label give us a real clue, also. If the final word is cheese, we know it is 100% cheese; if it says "cheese food", and watch for this—it is very common, we know it has a filler or something added; if it says "cheese spread," it's even less cheese; and "imitation processed cheese spread" is less yet.

Most cheeses freeze well, especially if you are going to grate them for cooking. Some crumble after being frozen. Colby is one of these.

Types of cheeses can be interchanged for many recipes. If mozzarella is expensive and Swiss is less, try Swiss on your pizza. It's really good and gets gooey and stringy like we like it.

Pizza can make a real nourishing meal if it's made with lots of good cheeses and served with a tossed salad and some good homemade grape juice (see food storage chapter). We like to get a family assembly line together and make up several at once to store in the freezer. Don't forget to make several small individual sizes, too. They sure come in handy.

Avoid the already grated and sliced cheeses. They are so much more expensive and don't keep as long either.

Eggs are another good protein source we don't want to overlook. They are also so versatile. Besides the usual fried, scrambled, and poached eggs for breakfast, everyone likes French toast. Try making it from thick sliced French bread and adding some nutmeg and a dash of sugar to your egg and milk mixture. The sugar helps it to brown nicely and the nutmeg adds that extra touch. Or try using orange juice in your egg mixture for another flavor treat. The little ones like to cut the bread out with cookie cutters first, makes the meal interesting! It's also fun to cut a circle from the middle of a slice of bread, lay the slice in your pan, and break an egg in the middle. This way you fry your toast and egg all at once.

It's a good idea always to keep a few hard boiled eggs on hand. This way they are always available for a quick snack. We have fun at our house writing funny sayings or drawing pictures on the eggs that are cooked. By the way, when you boil eggs—save the water! When it's cool, water your house plants, and I guarantee you'll have the prettiest green plants on the street. Every so often you can even crush the shells and cultivate this into the dirt around the plants. Sure does wonders!

Remember, there is a use for nearly everything. Even the plastic egg cartons, when washed thoroughly, are terrific for making extra ice cubes, freezing little batches of blended foods for baby, or, a little trick we enjoy, freezing small amounts of leftover fruit: half a banana, half a peach, or a few berries, etc., that have been mashed. We freeze each of these in a cube in the egg carton. Then, when it's frozen, we pop it out, wrap it in plastic wrap, and put it into our plastic bag for milk shakes. Whenever we want a milk shake, we pick our fruit choice and drop that cube, along with some milk and ice cream, into the blender, and instantly, the fruit shake of our choice!

When buying eggs always keep the figure "7" in your mind. If there is a difference of *less* than 7¢, always go to the next bigger size. However, if the price spread is *more* than 7¢, stay with the smaller ones. That way you are sure of getting the most egg for your money. Don't be concerned about the color of the yolk. If the yolk is deep yellow, it merely means the chicken has been eating lots of green grass, etc. If it is pale yellow, she has eaten more dry grains. Also, the color of the shell has no effect on the eggs. We get so tickled at my mother who won't eat a brown shelled egg. Really they are no different nutritionally. In cooking eggs of any kind, never use a high heat as it makes them tough.

With the many types of foods available, let's stretch our meat dollars even farther. Remember, too, that we are counseled to eat meat sparingly.

Chapter V

Convenience Foods and Mixes

If there is any place in your food budget you can trim dollars in a hurry, it is in the convenience food category. The nice part about saving here is it's lots of fun, rewarding, and, even nicer, it's usually just as "convenient". For two reasons, we have a policy in our home never to buy things that are "pre" put together, one reason being that we can nearly always put it together less expensively. The other reason being that, if we put it together, we will know exactly what is in it without a lot of additives, fillers, and artificial coloring and ingredients we don't really care to eat for our good health's sake. Let's discuss a few of these things.

First, don't just echo the word "convenience" in your mind because the label says so. It's interesting to see that the little "boil in bags" vegetables with butter and seasonings added are supposed to be "convenient" but it takes three minutes less time to cook a plain box of frozen vegetables! Who can't add a dab of butter and some salt and pepper in less than three minutes? That's not convenient in my book!

Don't be misled by fancy names. They may sound enticing but many are things that we would ordinarily throw away in our kitchens. For instance, the crumb mixture for meats is merely glorified bread crumbs with some seasonings added, and the stuffing mixes and croutons for salads are the same. Starting right now, keep a plastic bag in your freezer and, when there is half a piece of toast left over, put it in the bag. The same with one dry hot dog bun or the half of the hamburger bun mother wouldn't eat because she was dieting. If no one in your house likes the "heels", put them in, too. It won't take many days until you accumulate a nice supply of bread products. Then you are ready to make a nice bread pudding with lots of raisins, milk and eggs.

BREAD PUDDING

Combine in baking dish:

5 cups bread crumbs
4 cups scalded milk with
 1 stick margarine
1 cup sugar
4 beaten eggs
1/2 tsp. salt
1 tsp. cinnamon
1 tsp. nutmeg
1 cup raisins

Bake at 350° with pan of water beneath for 45 minutes or until knife comes out clean.

Serve warm with lemon or chocolate sauce.

Or a good stuffing for supper:

DELICIOUS BREAD STUFFING

Melt 2 sticks margarine.

Add:

3/4 cup onion (chopped)
1-1/2 cups celery (chopped)

Cook until transparent.

Add:

12 cups bread cubes
1 T. salt
1 tsp. pepper
1 T. sage

Mix well. Makes enough for a 12 lb. turkey or serve with other meats.

You don't have to have chicken or turkey to enjoy stuffing. Try it rolled in a round steak and baked, then slice and Yum! What a treat! Or try it with baked fish or just about any meat. It's also delicious to bake along side a pork roast or with browned pork chops laid on top. You can also dry your leftover breads on a cookie sheet in a slow oven until they are crisp and make your own croutons or crumb mixtures for meats. Just think how much money you'll be saving, how inventive you'll feel, and you'll also know that your family is eating much better.

Be careful of pictures on prepared foods. I have yet to find as glorious, delicious a dinner waiting under any of those wrappers as is pictured on the package. Analyze some of the dishes such as meat pies where you may think you are getting an adequate meal. A meat pie usually consists of two or three small bites of meat, four or five tiny chunks of vegetables, and the rest is filler such as gravy or crust. I'm sure anyone would admit that that's a poor excuse for a meal. Besides, why not mix up a bunch of good healthy meat pies or casserole dishes when you get a good buy on that roast. It's fun and so much more nutritious. The same is true for things like spaghetti and macaroni and cheese. I always follow the rule that if the food processors can freeze it to sell to me, why can't I freeze it myself? We pay so much extra for them to throw a few things together or add a few seasonings to something, and many times the convenience foods we buy are the same as what we threw away a few days ago as leftovers.

Let me share a story of one of the women who was in one of my food storage classes. One evening she rushed home to prepare supper. In a hurry, she stopped in at the grocery store to buy something "convenient". She saw a can of "beans and franks" so, remembering the ad on TV that talked about it being quick, she purchased that. She felt at the time it was a little expensive but . . . it was convenient. As she heated the beans she noticed there were only five small slices of franks in it. But her most upsetting discovery . . . When she opened the refrigerator to get lettuce for a tossed salad, there on a plate were three franks, left over from another meal! She always had pork and beans on her storage shelf downstairs, so she could have fixed her own beans and franks, in the same amount of time, having more meat in them and saving a considerable amount of money. Don't let yourself fall into this trap.

39

As you finish a meal, if you find you have about one good serving of everything left, take an aluminum pie pan and make your own TV dinner. Cover it tightly with foil and label it. Then some evening when you are rushed, let the family play "restaurant" and everyone choose the dinner of his choice. The kids love to make menus and play waiter and waitress on a night like this.

You know, we can buy french toast, waffles, and pancakes all frozen now. Why not freeze our own? We all nearly always have pancakes, waffles, etc. left over. Slip them in a bag and freeze them. It's great for that morning when someone oversleeps and breakfast is all cleaned up. The sleepyhead can just pop one in the toaster and it's ready to go.

Speaking of pancakes and waffles, why buy expensive mixes that really aren't so good when you can just as easily mix up some delicious ones of your own. There are none to compare with "Maxine Blotter's Pancakes".

MAXINE BLOTTER'S PANCAKES
Mix together:
2 cups flour (part whole wheat, part white)
2 cups buttermilk
1/4 cup oil
4 eggs
Dash of salt
2 tsp. soda
1 tsp. baking powder
Mix well and they're ready to go!

As I mentioned earlier, we like to keep several pizzas frozen and ready to cook. Let me share with you some of our other sandwich ideas that are fun to have made up, frozen, and ready for a quick snack.

Our favorite is to spread a hot dog bun lightly with mustard, add a frankfurter, chopped onions, and drained sauerkraut, then cover with "hot" chili, and sprinkle with grated cheese. Wrap these in foil and all you have to do is heat it through in the oven when you're ready.

Another great one is to fry tortillas in fat on both sides until they are crisp. Spread them all with a tortilla filling, sprinkle with grated cheese and chopped onion, and freeze. Then when you want them, lay them on a cookie sheet in the oven and heat them through, put them on your serving plate, cover them with shredded lettuce, and you're ready for our "Sunday Night Mexican Delight".

Don't pass up a chance to try our "Bean Sandwich Deluxe". Start with a toasted slice of bread, butter it, and spread it lightly with mustard. Spread with baked beans, a slice of cheese, onion if desired, and a crisp slice of bacon. Wrap these in foil, also, and freeze. For a quick summer supper, heat and serve your Bean Sandwich Deluxe with fresh tomato slices and celery sticks. In the winter it's great with a bowl of stewed tomatoes or tomato soup and carrot and celery sticks.

You can also make and freeze Reuben sandwiches, Heros, or about any combination you desire. Just avoid mayonnaise and lettuce. Mashed avocado and bacon bits on whole wheat bread is terrific frozen and packed in a lunch box or the picnic basket. Take along a fresh tomato from the garden and you'll really have a treat.

With a small amount of effort and a lot of family fun, you can have your own convenience counter as near as your freezer. The money you save will amaze you, and feeling better with good food will please you.

Another way you can save is on prepared salad dressings. These are all so easy to mix up ourselves with very little effort in an empty fruit bottle. They taste so much better and at a fraction of the cost. Please try some of the ones my family enjoy:

FRENCH DRESSING

Combine in quart jar and shake well:

1/4 cup water
1/2 cup vinegar
1-1/2 cups salad oil
1 can tomato soup
2 tsp. Worcestershire sauce
1/2 cup sugar
1 tsp. salt
1 tsp. pepper
1 tsp. table mustard
1/2 tsp. powdered garlic

POPPY SEED DRESSING

Combine in pint jar:

1/3 cup sugar
1/4 cup salad oil
2/3 cup Miracle Whip

Add as many poppy seeds as desired and fill jar with cream. Shake well.

THOUSAND ISLAND DRESSING

Combine:

1 cup Miracle Whip
1/4 cup catsup
1 hard-boiled egg (chopped)
1 onion (finely chopped)
1/3 cup olives (chopped)
1 tsp. table mustard
1/4 cup green pepper (chopped)
1/2 cup celery (chopped)

Mix well.

ROQUEFORT DRESSING

Combine in pint jar:

1/2 cup salad oil
1/2 cup water
4 or 8 oz. blue cheese (crumbled)

Fill jar with Miracle Whip. Shake well.

There are so many ice cream toppings and pancake-type syrups and toppings on the market, and these, too, sell for much more than it costs us to whip them up ourselves. Try your hand at some of these:

GRANDMA'S MAPLE SYRUP

Stir together:
4 cups white sugar
1/2 cup brown sugar
2 cups water

Cover and simmer for 10 minutes.

Remove from heat and add:
1 tsp. vanilla
1 tsp. maple flavoring

RASPBERRY SYRUP

Mix together:
1 pkg. frozen raspberries
2 cups sugar
1/2 cup water

Bring all ingredients to a boil.

(This also may be done with frozen strawberries.)

APPLE SYRUP

Mix together:
1 cup apple juice
2 cups sugar
1 cinnamon stick

Bring all ingredients to a boil.

HOT FUDGE SAUCE

In saucepan, combine:
1-1/2 cups sugar
6 T. cocoa
dash of salt
3 T. water

Add and bring to boil:
1 large can evaporated milk

Boil 4-5 minutes - until thickened.

Remove from heat and add:
4 T. butter
2 tsp. vanilla

As you happily work around your kitchens, you can sing this little theme song in regard to convenience foods:

*"Anything you can make,
we can make better!"*

And you can drop those saved pennies in the piggy bank!

Chapter VI

Simple But Scrumptious Baked Goods

The most exciting chapter to me in any book on food is the one on baking. As my friends and neighbors can tell you, this is the part I'm most anxious to share with you because it's what I enjoy doing most. I have had the good fortune of knowing many good cooks as we have moved around the country with my husband's company. I always have my ears to the ground (and nose in the oven!) for a good recipe. I'm sure my friends won't mind me sharing the ones we've gleaned for our family.

Let's start with cookies. From now on you won't even push your basket down the aisle of cookies and sweets at the grocery store. Homemade is always better, and better for you.

A few hints on cookies: always underbake them a minute or two. Take them out of the oven just before you think you should. They will be so much better. Also, try adding a little extra flour (about 1/4 cup to a 2 cup recipe and 1/2 cup to a 4 cup recipe.) I'm sure you'll be pleased with the nice rounded cookie you will get. Always put them to cool on an absorbent paper, such as newspaper, a paper sack, or paper toweling (but you have to buy paper towels, so why not use one of the other two?) When you do this, you'll notice the grease rings that the cookies leave. This is good because it will help your cookies stay fresh longer and not get a stale and rancid taste, (if they last that long!).

Don't panic if you are ready to bake cookies and the margarine is frozen. Merely get out your food grater and grate into your bowl. It will cream up so nicely with your sugar with no waiting!

When you are adding raisins to your cookies, put them on the cutting board and chop them slightly with the butcher knife. They are much nicer in your cookies. If you're adding nuts, chop them together too.

Never feel you must run to the store if a recipe calls for buttermilk or sour milk. Just add a good tablespoon of lemon juice or vinegar to a cup of milk. It's a lot cheaper, too, to use three tablespoons of cocoa and one tablespoon of shortening instead of a square of unsweetened chocolate.

In any of your baking, try not to use shiny pans. You get much nicer results from a dull or dark one. Also, remember when baking in glass to lower the temperature 25°. This really can make a difference in the end result.

The first cookie recipe I want to share with you is one I'm most proud of. It's an old German recipe from my Grandmother Scheel. I really treasure it. They just melt in your mouth and are so easy and economical to make.

GRANDMA SCHEEL'S BUTTER COOKIES

Beat together:
2 sticks margarine
1 cup sugar

Add:
2 egg yolks
Pinch of salt

Then add:
1-1/2 tsp. soda
1-1/2 tsp. lemon extract
2-1/2 cups flour

Mix together. Form balls the size of walnuts. Dip top side in sugar. Press flat with fork. Bake at 350° for 8-10 minutes.

Here are some other family favorites that are guaranteed to make your mouth water!

MAXINE'S COWBOY COOKIES

Beat together:
1 cup white sugar
1 cup brown sugar
1 cup shortening

Add:
2 eggs

Add:
2 cups flour
1 tsp. soda
1/2 tsp. salt
1/2 tsp. baking powder

Then add:
1 tsp. vanilla
2 cups oatmeal
1 small package chocolate chips

Mix together. Drop by spoonfuls onto cookie sheet. Bake at 375° for 8-10 minutes.

TENDER OATMEAL COOKIES

Simmer 1 cup raisins and 1 cup water in saucepan over low heat until raisins are plump (20-30 minutes). Drain raisin liquid into measuring cup. Add enough water to make 1/2 cup.

Cream:
3/4 cup shortening
1-1/2 cups sugar
2 eggs
1 tsp. vanilla

Stir in:
Raisin liquid

Then add together:
2-1/2 cups flour
1/2 tsp. baking powder
1 tsp. soda
1 tsp. salt
1 tsp. cinnamon
1/2 tsp. cloves

Add:
2 cups rolled oats
Raisins
1/2 cup chopped nuts

Drop rounded spoonfuls about 2 inches apart on ungreased cookie sheet. Bake at 400° for 8-10 minutes.

ROY'S SANDWICH COOKIES

Beat together:
3/4 cup margarine
1 cup sugar

Add:
1 egg

Add alternately:
1/4 cup milk
1/2 tsp. vanilla

and

2 cups flour
1 tsp. baking powder
1/2 tsp. soda
1/2 tsp. salt
3/4 cup cocoa

Mix together and chill. Shape into two rolls and chill again. Slice and bake as refrigerator cookies. Bake at 325° for 10 minutes. When cool, form a "sandwich" with this delicious mint frosting between two cookies:

Mint frosting

Mix together:
3 T. margarine
1-1/2 cup powdered sugar
3 T. milk
Green food coloring
Mint extract

The favorite dessert with the men in our house is pie. This is really such a fast, easy dessert to make, and yet it's the one most new brides are afraid of. I can see why they feel this way as I eat pies that have a crust like cardboard.

Please try this simple recipe and see how easy it can be to make tender flaky crust.

EASY PIE CRUST

(Two crust pie)

Mix together:
2 cups flour
1 tsp. salt

Stir in with fork:
2/3 cup oil

Sprinkle over and stir in with fork:
3 T. cold water

Mix together and roll out between two sheets of plastic wrap. Peel off plastic wrap and fit in pie pan. Bake at 450° for single crust and at 425° for double crust.

Pie shells will keep on the shelf for a week or two so always have one on hand. Another crust recipe that I especially enjoy for meat pies is this one:

LOIS'S PASTRY

Mix in large bowl:
2 cups flour
1 tsp. salt

Blend in small bowl:
3/4 cup shortening
1 egg yolk
1 T. lemon juice

Add to flour mixture and blend with fork till crumbly. Add 1/4 cup cold water and stir with fork till mixture makes a ball. Roll out as above and bake. (Makes one double - two single crusts.)

Now for all the goodies that go in the shell! Our first choice is pumpkin, and this recipe beats any one we've tasted:

NYE'S PUMPKIN PIE

Beat together:
1 large (29 oz.) can pumpkin
1 tsp. salt
3-1/2 cups milk
5 eggs
1-1/3 cups white sugar
2-1/2 tsp. cinnamon
1 tsp. ginger
1 tsp. nutmeg
1/2 tsp. cloves

Pour into three (3) unbaked pie shells. Bake at 425° for 45 minutes or until knife comes out clean.

Strawberry pie is so impressive yet so easily done the way we make it. We've named this one after Heidi's good friend, who always counts on her to bake him one for his birthday or when he visits us.

TOM'S STRAWBERRY PIE

Prepare 1 package Strawberry Danish Dessert as directed for pie filling.

Add 1 pint cut up fresh strawberries.

Pour into baked pie shell. Top with whipped cream.

The cream pies are also very easy to do. My girls would vote for banana or coconut cream over any other.

BANANA CREAM PIE

Cover bottom and sides of baked pie shell with banana slices. Pour into shell one recipe vanilla pudding or one package instant pudding. Top with whipped cream.

COCONUT CREAM PIE

Toast coconut in slow oven. Prepare vanilla pudding as above. Stir in 1/2 cup toasted coconut. Pour into baked pie shell. Top with whipped cream and sprinkle with more toasted coconut.

The best rhubarb pie is one from a dear friend of ours in Nebraska. This one is doubly good because it has a fantastic meringue that you can also use on a lemon or butterscotch pie.

My favorite (I guess because it's so fattening!) is "Delicious Pecan Pie". It's a never fail recipe and is the most delicious, melt-in-your-mouth, rich goody you ever tasted.

MILLIE'S SO GOOD RHUBARB PIE

Cook together until tender:
2 T. butter
2 cups diced rhubarb
1/2 cup white sugar
1/2 cup brown sugar

Add and cook until thick:
1/4 cup sugar
2 T. cornstarch
2 beaten egg yolks
Dash of salt
1/4 cup milk

Cool and pour into baked pie shell.

DELICIOUS PECAN PIE

Mix well:
1 cup dark corn syrup
1 cup brown sugar
1/3 tsp. salt
1/3 cup melted margarine
1 tsp. vanilla

Add 3 slightly beaten whole eggs.

Pour into unbaked pie shell and sprinkle 1-1/2 cups shelled whole pecans over all. Bake at 350° for 45 minutes.

PERFECT MERINGUE

Dissolve 1 T. cornstarch in 1 T. cold water. Add 1/2 cup water and cook until thick and clear. Cool thoroughly. Beat 3 egg whites until foamy; add 6 T. sugar and beat until stiff. Add cooled mixture to beaten egg whites and spread on pie. Bake at 350° until brown (12-15 minutes).

A family specialty is "Mom's Sour Cream Pie". This dates back to my childhood on the farm in Nebraska. The spicy aroma of this pretty pie coming from the oven could bring hayers in out of the field in a hurry.

MOM'S SOUR CREAM PIE

Mix together:
2 cups sour cream
1 cup sugar
2 T. flour
2 tsp. cinnamon
1/2 tsp. cloves
1 cup raisins
4 egg yolks

Pour into an unbaked pie shell and bake at 350° for 30 minutes. Cool, then add meringue and brown.

Cakes are fun to mix up, and you can have so much variety and creativity that I can't imagine why anyone would resort to a box mix. It sure isn't any easier, and it's much less rewarding. I guess people's apprehension in cake baking goes back to the days when it was such a tedious effort to obtain good results. That has all changed, and with all the fool proof recipes anyone can whip one up as easily as a mix.

The most delicious chocolate cake you ever tasted is this one from a friend of ours in Kansas City. It is so moist and delicious, you don't even need icing. It's terrific for lunch boxes.

DELICIOUS CHOCOLATE CAKE

Beat together:
1 cup salad oil
1 cup buttermilk
2 egg yolks
1 tsp. vanilla

Add:
2 cups sugar
2 cups flour
1/2 cup cocoa
1 T. soda
1/4 tsp. salt

Add:
1 cup boiling water

Bake in 9x12 inch pan or 3 round pans at 325° for one hour.

Nothing could be easier than this next cake. It, too, is nice and moist and doesn't require an icing. We like this one for picnics or on a fall evening with a cup of hot cider.

APPLE TORTE CAKE

Cream:
2 cups sugar
1 stick margarine

Add:
2 eggs

Beat well and add:
4 cups grated apples

Add:
2 cups flour
2 tsp. soda
2 tsp. cinnamon
1/2 tsp. nutmeg
1 cup nuts (chopped)

Bake in 9x13 inch pan at 350° for 45 minutes. Refrigerate.

The next recipe is my all-time favorite. I take it everywhere. It's kind of a cross between a cake and brownies. It is so economical (costs about half as much to make as brownies), and it's a hit with everyone!

COCOA BARS

Beat together:
1 stick margarine
1 cup sugar
1 egg

Add:
3/4 cup sour milk
1 tsp. vanilla

Then add:
1-1/2 cups flour
1/2 tsp. soda
1/2 tsp. salt
1/2 cup cocoa

Bake in greased 9x12 inch pan at 350° for 20-25 minutes. Frost with chocolate icing and sprinkle with chopped nuts.

Of course, we all love good, rich brownies. This is the best recipe I've tasted.

PAULINE'S BROWNIES

Melt 2 sticks margarine and add 10 T. cocoa. Then add 2 cups sugar and beat well.

Add:
4 eggs (beaten)
1-1/2 cup flour
Dash of salt

Mix well and stir in nuts. Spread in 9x12 inch greased pan. Bake at 350° for 25-30 minutes.

This cake also falls into the category of not needing icing. It's so delicious eaten plain, but it's even better with a scoop of ice cream on the side.

CHOCO-DATE CAKE

Combine 1 cup chopped dates and 1 cup boiling water. Cool to room temperature.

Stir 2/3 cup shortening to soften; gradually add 1 cup sugar, creaming until fluffy. Blend in 1 tsp. vanilla, add 2 eggs, one at a time, beating well after each addition.

Sift together 1-3/4 cups flour, 2 T. cocoa, 1 tsp. soda, 1/2 tsp. salt. Add to creamed mixture alternately with date mixture, beating after each addition. Spread in greased 9x13 inch pan. Sprinkle 1 cup chocolate chips and 1 cup chopped nuts on top. Bake at 350° for 40-45 minutes or until done. Cool in pan. Cut in squares and top with whipped cream.

Our freezer is hardly ever without this satisfying "Spicy Pumpkin Loaf". We always take several loaves along as we travel. It's moist, delicious, not too sweet, and not messy to eat in the car. It's so good with a thermos of cold milk or juice.

SPICY PUMPKIN LOAF

Combine:
3-3/4 cups flour
2 tsp. soda
2 tsp. cinnamon
1 tsp. salt
1 tsp. nutmeg
1/2 tsp. ginger
1/2 tsp. ground cloves
Cream:
2 sticks margarine
Gradually add:
2 cups sugar—cream well.

Blend in and beat well:
4 eggs

At low speed, add dry ingredients alternately with 1-1/2 cups canned or cooked pumpkin, beginning and ending with dry ingredients.

Stir in 12 oz. pkg. chocolate chips and 1 cup chopped nuts.

Turn into two greased 9x5 inch loaf pans. Bake at 350° for 1 hour. Cool, then drizzle with the delicious spice glaze (below). Slices better after a day.

Spice glaze
Combine:
1 cup powdered sugar
1/4 tsp. nutmeg
1/4 tsp. cinnamon
Dash of cloves

Blend in:
3-4 T. hot water until the consistency of a glaze.

My daughter Kristen's first choice is always carrot cake. There are so many versions of this cake, but the very best comes from our dear friend from New Zealand.

JENET'S CARROT CAKE

Mix together:
3 cups flour
2 tsp. baking powder
2 tsp. baking soda
2 tsp. cinnamon
1/2 tsp. salt

In another bowl, toss together:
1 cup raisins
1/2 cup coarsely chopped nuts

Take 2 T. of above flour mixture and toss with raisins and nuts.

In another large mixing bowl, beat:
2 cups sugar
1-1/2 cups corn oil
1 tsp. vanilla

Then thoroughly beat in:
4 eggs

Stir in dry ingredients alternately with 3 cups finely grated carrots and blend until smooth.

Add nut-raisin mixture and mix well. Pour in greased angel cake pan. Bake at 350° for 1-1/4 hours (approx.) until top springs back to touch. Cool on wire rack for 10 minutes, then top with this cheese frosting.

Cream cheese frosting

Mix until blended:
1 pkg. (3 oz.) cream cheese—soft
2 T. light corn syrup

Add:
2-1/4 cups powdered sugar
2 tsp. vanilla

Stir until smooth.

Both "Date-Nut Bread" and the "Banana Bread" in Chapter 2 are favorites at our house. Everyone enjoys them as much as a sweeter cake. They freeze so well and are really handy to have on hand.

DATE-NUT BREAD

Combine and let cool:
1-1/2 cups boiling water
1-1/2 cups chopped dates

Mix together:
1/2 cup packed brown sugar
1 T. shortening
1 egg
Add date mixture.

Then add:
2-1/4 cups flour
1 tsp. soda
1/2 tsp. salt

Mix and add chopped nuts.

Bake at 350° for 60-70 minutes in large loaf pan.

Several of the desserts we enjoy that don't fall under the heading of cakes and pies are so good we have to share them with you, too.

Of course, number one would have to be my "Down-in-the-Dumps Pudding". This has truly become a family tradition. I'm afraid I'm a real chocolate lover and when I'm feeling low or "down-in-the-dumps", nothing makes me feel better than to indulge myself in something chocolate and gooey. I started making this very rich, good dessert and really enjoyed a big helping on one particularly depressing day. It soon became automatic; when someone in the family came in the house and smelled this heavenly delight baking, they called out "Oh! Oh! Mom's down-in-the-dumps!" and we'd all have a good laugh. Give it a try! Eat it warm from the oven with a scoop of ice cream! It works wonders!

DOWN-IN-THE-DUMPS PUDDING

Beat together:
2 cups flour
1-1/2 cups sugar
4 tsp. baking powder
1/2 tsp. salt
4 T. cocoa

Stir in:
1 cup milk
4 T. vegetable oil
2 cups chopped nuts

Spread mixture in ungreased 9x13 inch pan.

Blend in small bowl:
2 cups brown sugar (packed)
1/2 cup cocoa

Sprinkle over top of batter.

Pour over all: 3-1/2 cups hot water.
Bake at 350° for 45 minutes.

We like to enjoy lots of apples in the fall, and when we tire of pies and cakes, this is a delicious change. It's so easy. It, too, is very best when served warm with ice cream.

APPLE MACAROON

Fill pie pan with 4 medium apples sliced.

Sprinkle with:
1/2 cup sugar
1/2 tsp. cinnamon
1/2 cup chopped nuts

Beat:
2 eggs

Add:
1/2 cup sugar
1 cup flour
1 stick margarine (melted)

Mix together and pour dough over apples. Bake at 300° for 1-1/2 hours.

Rhubarb is another well-liked fruit in our house so, in the spring, we enjoy this dessert real often.

DONNA'S RHUBARB DESSERT

Mix together like pie crust:
2 cups flour
3/4 cup powdered sugar
1 cup margarine

Press into 9x13 inch pan and bake at 350° for 15 minutes.

Beat together:
4 eggs
3 cups sugar
1-1/2 tsp. salt

Add:
4 cups chopped rhubarb
1/2 cup raisins

Put this mixture on top of crust and bake for 45 minutes longer.

Whenever we're having a special occasion, the first dessert the kids request is always our "Date Delight". Two interesting things about this recipe are the fact that it doesn't taste a bit like dates, and it was passed on to me by a sweet friend in Omaha who's name is also "Delight". It is so good, I guarantee you'll eat more than you should!

DATE DELIGHT

Bring to boil:
1 cup chopped dates
3/4 cup water
1/4 tsp. salt

Simmer for 3 minutes and add 2 cups small marshmallows. Cool.

Add:
1/2 cup chopped pecans

Crush 14 Oreos. Spread 1/2 of crumbs in 10x6x1-1/2 inch pan. Spread date mixture over cookie crumbs.

Whip 1 cup cream—spread over date mixture.

Sprinkle with the rest of the crumbs. Then sprinkle with chopped pecans. Chill overnight.

No visit to Grandma Boldt's house is complete without her yummy raisin bars. We make them often at home, but somehow they are always more fun to eat at Grandma's. By the way, they freeze well, too.

MOM'S RAISIN BARS

Mix together:
1 cup butter
1-3/4 cup oatmeal
1 tsp. soda
1 cup brown sugar
1-3/4 cups flour
1/2 tsp. salt

Pat half of mixture into greased 9x13 inch pan.

Mix together:
3 T. flour
2 cups chopped raisins
3/4 cup sugar
1-1/4 cup hot water
Juice of 1/2 lemon

Cook until thick and pour over mixture in pan. Lightly pat rest of the dry ingredients on top of raisin mixture. Bake at 350° for 40 minutes.

Now for the most fun and rewarding baking you'll ever do—yeast doughs! I love working with these because they are so versatile and exciting. I firmly believe you should have different recipes for each of the different types of dough, such as breads, dinner rolls, and sweet rolls. Each has its own little niche or personality, and something is lost in making rolls out of bread dough, etc. Each also has specific ingredients for its particular behavior.

You will be surprised and pleased, I hope, to notice that none of my yeast doughs require kneading. This is a never fail remedy for beginning cooks who often use too much or too little flour or are not sure about the kneading process.

Anyone can enjoy these recipes without a lot of practice. Many novices at cooking, who have taken my classes and used these recipes, are receiving compliments and praise from their families. Many of their husbands won't let them buy any more baked goods because theirs are so good.

Let's start first with the basic never fail bread recipe. This can be varied about as many ways as you can think of. When I mix up a batch, I often change it to "honey wheat bread" by substituting honey for the sugar and using 1/2 whole wheat flour and 1/2 white flour. Sometimes I layer in some cinnamon and sugar mixture and chopped raisins. This makes terrific "morning toast". Other times, to make a "seeded bread", I brush it with egg white and sprinkle it with sesame or poppy seeds. I also roll small (size of a walnut) pieces between my floured hands to make long, little sticks. These I brush with egg white and sprinkle with minced garlic and parmesan cheese. These "garlic sticks" are great with spaghetti.

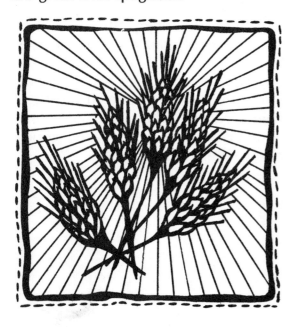

EASY NO KNEAD BREAD

In large bowl, pour 5 cups warm water. Add 2 pkgs. dry yeast.

When yeast is ready, add:
8 T. sugar or honey
8 T. shortening
8 tsp. salt
6 cups flour

Beat on high speed for 3 minutes.

Add:
6 more cups of flour.

Stir in with spoon. Let rise. Spoon into pans. Let rise again. Bake at 375° for 45 minutes in large pans, 30 minutes in small. Take from pans immediately, brush with butter, and let cool on racks. Makes 4 large loaves or 7 small loaves.

Everyone will receive verbal bouquets for these fantastic melt-in-your-mouth rolls. I promise even you will be overwhelmed with their goodness. They are terrific for Sunday dinner because you can mix them up Friday or Saturday and just roll them out Sunday morning. When you get home from Sunday School, they are ready to pop into the oven.

MELT-IN-YOUR-MOUTH DINNER ROLLS

Dissolve 1 pkg. yeast in 1/2 cup warm water.

Add:
1 T. sugar
1 tsp. Baking powder

Let stand for 20 minutes.

Scald 1 cup milk.

Add:
1/3 cup margarine
1/3 cup sugar
Dash of salt

Cool, then add 2 beaten eggs.

Combine all with 4-1/2 cups flour. Cover and refrigerate overnight. Roll out 2 hours before serving. Bake at 425° for 10 minutes. (Shape either as butterhorns or as pinwheels in muffin pans).

There is nothing like hot yummy German scones to keep your family or guests coming back for more. I really enjoy this recipe because I can mix it up and keep it in the frige for a week or two. Then when unexpected guests drop in or the kids come home starving, it only takes a few minutes to serve a fabulous treat.

We like to arrange on the table several bowls of jams and honey and, of course, Grandma's sugar bowl, which is traditional at our house for dipping scones. Then, as fast as I can fry them, everyone dips their own and enjoys!

GERMAN SCONES

Dissolve 2 pkgs. yeast in 1/2 cup warm water. Add 1 T. sugar.

Pour 1 cup boiling water over:
1/2 cup sugar
1/2 cup margarine
2 tsp. salt

Add:
3 beaten eggs
Yeast mixture
2 cups flour

Beat with mixer until smooth. Add 2-1/2 cups flour and stir in. Let rise for 1 hour, then refrigerate. When desired, roll out very thin and cut in 2 inch squares. Fry in hot fat.

After you've tried your hand at these yeast doughs, move on to some delicious sweet rolls. This recipe, again, is never fail, and you can have so much pleasure creating goodies for your family. Here is the basic recipe:

SWEET ROLLS

Dissolve 1 pkg. yeast in 1/4 cup warm water.

Mix together:
1 cup scalded milk
1 stick margarine (melted)
1/2 cup sugar
1-1/2 tsp. salt

Add:
Yeast mixture
3 beaten eggs
4-3/4 cup flour

Mix together and let rise.

Sweet Roll Variations

For cinnamon rolls:

Roll out the dough in a rectangle. Sprinkle cinnamon mixture (1/2 cup sugar and 2 tsp. cinnamon) over dough. Roll up dough lengthwise and slice. Place rolls on greased cookie sheet and flatten to size of roll. Bake at 375° for 12-15 minutes. Let cool slightly and frost with powdered sugar glaze.

For caramel-pecan rolls:

To make caramel mixture, cook together for one minute:

1/3 cup butter
1/2 cup brown sugar
4 T. corn syrup

Place whole or chopped pecans in bottom of greased muffin cups. Drop in one spoonful of caramel mixture. Prepare dough as for cinnamon rolls. Put slices into muffin cups. Bake at 375° for 12-15 minutes. Immediately turn muffin pan onto platter to remove rolls and let cool.

Now that we've discussed the goodies we can treat our family with, let me give you just one little tip on our "waste not, want not" theme. Along with the plastic bag in your freezer in which you keep all the leftover bread products, keep another for sweet things: that half a cookie, piece of dried up cake, or hard doughnut. When you have a nice supply, crush them all together and layer the crumbs in a parfait glass with a simple pudding to make a delightful dessert. Or you can sprinkle them on top of a thickened fruit and add a little cinnamon and nutmeg for a tasty fruit cobbler. You'll have so much fun finding new things to do with these yummy crumbs. They're even good sprinkled over ice cream!

Happy baking!

Chapter VII
Grains for Goodness

I would like to take a little time, now, and talk with you about the grains and cereals in our daily diet. These are so important, and yet I'm afraid they are very poorly used. They can really add variety and interest to our meals if we learn about them and use them properly. The nice part is that they taste as good as they are good for us.

First, let's spend a minute on prepared breakfast cereals. Some noted nutritionists tell us that "never before have we bought so little food in such big boxes." I firmly believe this, and have you looked at the prices of the large boxes lately? That in itself is enough to make you change your buying habits. If your family consumes much of these packaged cereals, they really are getting very little but empty calories. Many of the cereals are doing us about as much good as eating styrofoam.

If you insist on buying these cereals with your vital food dollars, at least check the ingredients on the side panel. In many, sugar is the no. 1 or 2 ingredient. But the best way is to avoid them altogether—don't get caught up in the bad habit, and start utilizing some of the good foods for breakfast.

If you enjoy cold cereal in the morning, make your own granola. Granola is so simple to make, and you can vary it to suit your taste. Don't spend extra money buying it because it isn't any different from the other prepared cereals on the grocer's shelf. We especially enjoy this recipe. I make a large batch and keep quart jars of it in my freezer so it stays nice and fresh and retains all the good nutrients.

DELICIOUS GRANOLA

Spread 4 cups rolled oats on ungreased sheet cake pan and bake at 350° for 10 minutes.

Stir in:
1 cup flaked coconut
1 cup peanuts, coarsely chopped (or other type nuts)
3/4 cup wheat germ

Then add:
1/2 cup honey
1/3 cup vegetable oil
1 tsp. vanilla

Mix until dry ingredients are well-coated. Bake at 350° for 20-25 minutes, stirring occasionally to brown evenly.

Stir in:
1 pkg. (8 oz.) dried apricots, chopped
1 cup raisins

(Other dried fruit may be substituted for apricots or raisins.)

Try experimenting with the different grains available. Oats is one of the most popular. Remember the Gritvous we made in an earlier chapter? Try cooking the cut oats as cereal. They have lots more food value than the rolled oats. Also, as you cook your cereals, try adding a handful of raisins, currants, apple chunks and cinnamon, peach slices, or just about anything your family enjoys. Instead of sugar as your sweetener, try honey, molasses, or brown sugar. Nothing is so satisfying or leaves you with a better feeling than a steaming bowl of nutritious cooked cereal. Some people refer to any cooked cereal as mush! I have a real dislike for this term. It's a matter of psychology. It seems to me that the term would turn anyone off. It's amazing how what you call something can affect its desirability and the pleasure it brings to your family. I often give leftovers fun names, and we all enjoy it.

One of the most useful grains, I think, is corn. We all enjoy it as a vegetable, but let's consider corn meal. Corn meal is also enjoyable as a cereal. Our favorite way to use corn meal is in corn bread, to be enjoyed with butter, hot homemade maple syrup, and sausage. With a fresh fruit cup and a tall glass of cold milk, it's a mighty pleasing meal! This grain can be used in so many tasty ways in Mexican cooking, as I mentioned earlier. It is also excellent for dipping liver or fish for frying. Speaking of fish, nothing goes so well with it as cole slaw and "Hush Puppies". This is a meal we learned to love while living in Texas. They tell me that the old cowboys used to cook corn bread (or Johnny Cake) over the fire and , as their dogs howled and barked at the fragrant aroma, they would pinch off a piece and toss it to them, saying "Hush puppies!"

This is my favorite hush puppy recipe. It's great served with crispy fried fish or with a hot bowl of chili.

HUSH PUPPIES

Cook together:
1-1/2 cups corn meal
1-1/2 cups water

Cook for about 6 minutes, stirring until mixture is stiff and begins to form in ball. Remove from heat.

Add:
1/3 cup milk
1 T. oil
2 tsp. onion (chopped)

Stir until smooth.

Gradually add:
2 eggs (beaten)

Blend together:
1 cup flour
3 tsp. baking powder
2 tsp. salt
1 tsp. sugar (if desired)

Add dry ingredients to corn meal batter, mixing thoroughly.

Drop batter by teaspoonfuls into hot (375° - 1 inch deep) fat. Fry for 6-7 minutes. Drain.

The next grain we should give thought to is rice. This is also a very versatile and nutritious food. The ways to use it are almost limitless. A hot steaming bowl of rice with cream and sugar makes a good breakfast cereal. If you want to give your family a pleasant change, try making a yummy rice pudding for breakfast with lots of eggs, milk, raisins, cinnamon, and nutmeg. A large glass of orange juice and toast completes this tempting menu.

There are several types of rice. Be sure you try all of them. There are white, long grain, brown, and wild. Our favorite is brown because of its nutty-like taste. The wild rice is the most expensive but is a taste treat in itself.

Here are my two most used rice casseroles. They are very inexpensive and easy to make. Great for a covered dish supper or when unexpected guests drop in.

CHOW MEIN CASSEROLE

Brown:
1 lb. hamburger
2 chopped onions

Add (into pan):

1 can cream of mushroom soup
1 can cream of chicken soup
1-1/2 cups warm water

1/2 cup uncooked rice
1 T. soy sauce

Mix together and bake at 350° for 30 minutes covered and then 30 more minutes uncovered. Sprinkle with Chinese noodles and set back into oven for 3-4 minutes.

SPICY TEXAS CASSEROLE

Brown:
1 lb. hamburger

Add and brown a little longer:
3 large onions (chopped)
1 large green pepper (chopped)

Stir in:
2 cups cooked tomatoes
1/2 cup uncooked rice
2 tsp. chili powder
2 tsp. salt
1/8 tsp. pepper
Dash of garlic salt

Bake at 350° for 45 minutes with cover and another 15 minutes without cover.

Just a word about the rye grain. It has lots of vitamins and minerals and creates a pleasant change in our bread and rolls. It's a delicious combination for a sandwich of ham or roast that you have stored in the freezer. One thing to remember when working with rye flour is that it is very low in gluten, and you must use another type of flour with it.

One grain that is often overlooked is barley. The most common type is pearl barley. I love using this in vegetable and beef type soups. It's a good meat extender and gives us lots of different nutrients. Try it!

Of course, wheat is the grain that is considered the staff of our lives. Since this is an important grain and one we need to use in our every day life, I will cover it extensively in my next chapter on Food Storage.

Chapter VIII
Food Storage

This chapter is what this book is really all about. First of all, what is a food storage program? We have been counseled by the Lord, through our church leaders, to keep on hand a year's supply of food and necessities to sustain our family in time of need. This need could range from a job loss, truck or rail strike, national disaster, or the sickness or death of the breadwinner, or other family crisis. What wise counsel this is, and how invaluable it has proved to be to the many of us who have heeded this counsel. Need we ask ourselves why? 1) We have been counseled by the Lord, through a prophet; 2) The scriptures tell us in I Timothy 5:8 :

But if any provide not for his own, and specially for those of his own house, he hath denied the faith, and is worse than an infidel.

and 3) It's a known fact that foods "have their season". Every few years fruit trees don't bear, shortages occur, and the economy has its ups and downs. Remember the sugar shortage a few years ago?

Now that we are converted to the storage program, the question is asked "How?" "How" is exactly what I have been preparing you for in the previous chapters. By correcting your buying habits, avoiding "empty calorie" foods, avoiding convenience foods, and making your own mixes, you are saving dollars to apply to this program. You are also learning to make the foods you use daily from the foods stored on your shelves. You store the basics anyway, and by making your own mixes, you eliminate all these from your storage shelf, thus saving yourself money.

Remember, our bodies are the temples of our spirits, and we want to feed them properly. We also want to be able to eat nutritiously during times of need when we use our food storage. It is only feasible, then, to "Store what you eat and eat what you store."

There are so many fallacies and misconceptions about food storage. I would like to correct a few. First, please don't be misled into thinking, "If times get tough, we'll eat it." This just isn't so. Do you remember trying to encourage your family to eat something right before grocery day when there wasn't much in the house? They all have likes and dislikes and this really doesn't change. It is also important at crisis times to keep morale up. If hubby has lost his job, he will feel even worse if everyone is complaining about the food. It is crucial for us as homemakers to look ahead and foresee these things. If you are storing what you normally eat and utilizing these foods every day on your table, no one will feel the change as drastically. It is so comforting to know that you have, stored on your shelves, food for a year that your family would normally eat.

I really worry about families who store things for their food supply that they aren't accustomed to eating, such as the pre-packaged emergency dried foods. This would be fine if you used them all the time in your daily menus and your family were used to them. However, if your family plan on eating pre-packaged dried food for a year and their systems are not used to it, many health problems could result, and you'll be serving an unhappy family who don't care for the food.

The Lord has told us to use wisdom in all things. How logical it is, then, simply to store what we normally eat. This way, not only are we supplied for the year as we've been counseled, we also save food dollars every day by being able to take advantage of specials.

Let me show you how to get started and make your plan work. First, sit down with your family and make a list of the basic foods you use in a week. This is easy to do, taking the three meals a day, and it's not so overwhelming to comprehend.

Now, let's say you eat one can of vegetables a day for the seven days and twice that week you eat corn. Therefore, you need 104 cans of corn for the year (figuring 2 x 52). That would only be about four cases. As you get your weekly list figured, multiply each item by 52 and you'll have your needs. You'll find the figures aren't so staggering after all! Now remember, these are the basics—no unneeded frills! Besides, we can make our own treats from what we have and be healthier, too. Did you know, statistics show that 25-40 per cent of what most people put in their grocery carts are unnecessary, empty calories?

The next step is to prepare a place to keep your supply. Ideally, this should have a stable temperature of 55°-60°. However, if this is impossible, come as close as you can. Your storage area, of course, should be dry and, also, dark. Nearly everything keeps better if it is not exposed to light. Never store anything directly on a concrete floor, even boxes of canned goods. Always use some old lumber, bricks, or whatever, to raise your jars, cans, and boxes up off the floor.

There are no objections to using your freezer for part of your food storage. Just be sure you know how to process or handle the foods you've frozen if your freezer should go out. We'll discuss this in our drying and canning processes.

Now we are ready to start accumulating our foods. With our food list handy and foods listed in order of "most important first", let's begin. Let's say corn was no. 1. You needed 4 cases, so you start there. Don't use any of that corn until you have 4 cases; then, as you buy more, put it to the back of the shelf and slide the same amount to the front for use, always keeping the required number on the shelf. Do this with each item on your list. Soon you'll have your needed amount and will be able to use your grocery money each pay day to buy up only specials. This way you will constantly be saving money, you'll always have your year's supply, it will

always be fresh because of rotation, nothing will ever be much over a year old, you'll be following the counsel of the Lord, and you'll be eating wisely and healthily with no waste because you will only be storing what you eat. This way you can buy things in season and always take advantage of bargains.

I can't stress enough the peace of mind a year's food supply that's available for use at any time can give you. You can see that if your food storage were sealed away somewhere, you would not want to open it, so it wouldn't be available for short periods of necessity. Not only that, but after keeping your food for so many years not wanting to open it, you would probably end up throwing most of it away. What foolish logic and a waste of money.

Now that you have a buying plan, let's discuss how to store and use some of these foods, with the exception of fruits and vegetables. They're covered in Chapter 8. As members of The Church of Jesus Christ of Latter-day Saints, we nearly all store wheat, so let's begin there. I'm distressed at the number of people I meet in my classes who realize the importance of wheat storage but have no idea how to store or use their wheat. This, again, is an example of not saying "If times are rough enough, we'll survive." It is so foolish to invest so much of our food dollars in something, not know how to use it, and end up not enjoying it or having it make us sick. We need to introduce wheat to our digestive systems a little at a time. We become so accustomed to such refined foods that if we started eating wheat solely, it could cause problems in our health. We should keep a jar of wheat on our counter and use it daily now! We can benefit so much from its nutrients, and if we are going to store it, why not eat it? There are so many fun uses.

First, if you make sure the wheat you buy is clean hard winter wheat with less than 10% moisture and a protein content of above 11.5%, you will have no problem with storage. Just keep it dry and in a container with a tight lid (I use metal garbage cans). You can also rotate it from can to can every six months, and this discourages any bugs, etc. I keep one empty can on the end of my row of wheat cans, then every six months we pour the wheat from can to can, leaving the empty can on the opposite end. Of course, you'll be using your wheat constantly, so you'll never have a huge amount of old wheat to worry over.

You can do many things with your wheat without any expensive equipment. There are always lots of commercial gimmicks to spend our money on, but it's much more fun to do things with wheat using things you already have (saves dollars and makes sense!).

A good place to start is by steaming some of your wheat. Everyone has a pan of some sort that you can use as a steamer. Put water in the bottom of your pan and then set a container of wheat in the pan on a rack so the steam rises around it. I usually put 1/2 cup wheat in 2 cups water with 1/2 tsp. salt in my container, then enough water in the bottom of the steamer so it doesn't cook dry, put a lid on, and steam the wheat slowly overnight (for about 12 hours). It's so easy to put the wheat on to cook as you're cleaning up the supper dishes. Then, in the morning, it's cooked and ready for hot cereal. It's delicious with milk or cream and brown sugar or honey. If you don't use it all for breakfast, store it in a covered container in the refrigerator, and it makes the best, most nutritious and economical meat extender you ever had. I use it in chili, spaghetti sauce, meat loaf, casseroles, etc. Just mix it in with your ground meat. You can also use it in any recipe calling for cooked rice. It's really good, and, in many dishes, you don't even know it's there.

If you like cracked wheat cereal in the morning, start 2 cups water boiling with a dash of salt when you get up. Put 1/2 cup wheat kernels in your blender and blend them for a minute or two (however fine you like it), then stir them slowly into your boiling water with a wire whisk, and cook for about 10 minutes. Boy, is it good! Try a few added raisins, dried apples, peaches, etc.! Not only is it delicious and nutritious, but you can serve a family of six for about 2¢. Remember, never blend more than 1/2 cup wheat at a time, though. This is a recommended amount published by the blender companies.

You know, we can get all the needed nutrients from wheat except Vitamin C, and, by using a little ingenuity, we can even get that! Take that long, narrow, flat styrofoam meat tray you got at the grocery store, fill it with clean soil, plant a handful of wheat kernels, and cover them lightly with the soil. Now keep this on your kitchen window sill and spray with water several times a day, keeping it very moist. Soon you will have a pretty crop of wheat grass. When the grass reaches 3-4 inches, clip it regularly and add it to salads, muffin batter, soups, etc. Voilà!—our Vitamin C!

You can also place a handful of wheat kernels in a glass jar, cover the top with a piece of nylon net, secure the net with a rubber band, run water over the wheat, pour off the excess, and rotate the jar so the kernels cling to the sides. Place the jar on its side in a dark cupboard, then 2-3 times a day, dampen and rotate the jar. In 2-3 days you'll have healthy little sprouts. You can set it on your window for a day to green up; however, this isn't necessary. When the sprouts are about 1/2 inch long, just add kernels and all to your fresh green salads—it's great! And much more economical than croutons! I like to take a slice of whole wheat bread and spread it with butter, avocado, a tomato slice, and wheat sprouts. Oh, is that good! These sprouts are also good in muffin batter. You'll find oodles of ways to use them.

The pioneers even made chewing gum from their wheat. It's lots of fun. Take a small amount of wheat kernels and just start chewing. It will eventually turn into gum. As a child, we did this often at harvest time. After we got our gum made, we would soak it in cherry juice overnight, flavoring our gum! Try it some Family Night. I guarantee you lots of laughs!

A kernel of wheat is a very interesting little thing. It is covered with a skin, which is the bran and is very good for us. Then inside, it is filled with a white fluffy substance, which is in essence like a cotton filler. Hidden down in the corner is the wheat germ, which is chock full of vitamins and minerals and is very oily. When we buy white bread in the store, we are basically getting the "cotton filler" of the wheat, or styrofoam bread as my husband calls it. The wheat bread or flour on the store shelves could not even contain 100% of the wheat kernel without adding lots of preservatives because the oil in the wheat goes rancid. This is why it is so important as we grind our own wheat flour that we grind only a small amount at a time. If it sits for a long period of time, the air oxidizes the Vitamin E. We should keep the freshly ground flour in the refrigerator, or even the freezer if we are not going to use it up within a week or so.

The most common way of storing fruits and vegetables is by canning or bottling. This is a relatively easy process so, if you are a beginner, don't let it frighten you. One of the best feelings I know comes from looking at all our pretty bottles of food, lined up on the shelves just waiting to be enjoyed.

Nearly all fruits are acidic and are safe to can in the boiling water bath canner, as well as tomatoes. However, when canning vegetables and meats or any low acid food, always use a pressure canner. The simple directions come with both these pieces of equipment. Just follow directions! If you live in a higher altitude, be sure you check the proper adjustments.

All fruits will call for a sugar syrup, and this is so easy to remember:

Light syrup: 1 cup sugar -
   3 cups water

Medium syrup: 2 cups sugar -
   3 cups water

Heavy syrup: 3 cups sugar -
   3 cups water

Dissolve the sugar in water and bring to a boil. Pour the boiling liquid over fruit in jars.

We prefer the light syrup. The fruit is much more tasty, and it is much more economical and better for you, too.

Now for some fun ideas with canning.

When I can my applesauce, I leave the apples quite chunky and add a generous amount of cinnamon and nutmeg to the sugar. We enjoy it most this way as applesauce, and if I'm in a hurry, I can use it as apple pie filling because of the nice chunks!

I always can some blueberries and other available berries in bottles in light sugar syrup. This is so delicious on hot cakes when it's heated.

Don't forget to try the mock cherries and minted pears I mentioned in the chapter on buying fruits and vegetables.

It is nice to can some rhubarb sauce, in addition to what you freeze. Rhubarb sauce is always handy and makes a tasty treat with some cookies after school or with a warm coffee cake for breakfast.

Of course, peaches are available in most places and very easy to can. No fruit shelf is complete without those sparkling, golden halves and slices in their jars. Try putting one peach pit in each jar for a little added color and flavor. It really makes a difference.

No one would want to leave out the pickling in the summer time. Two pickle recipes we are never without are these two from my mother's farm in Nebraska.

SWEET PICKLES

Cover 72 cucumbers with cold water and 1 cup salt. Let stand for one week. Then, for three consecutive mornings pour off water and pour on fresh boiling water (keeping the cucumbers covered). On 2nd morning add 1 T. alum and split the large cucumbers.

Heat 5 cups vinegar, 5 cups sugar, 1/2 oz. celery seed and pour over pickles. Reheat for three mornings then pack in jars and seal.

NEVER FAIL DILL PICKLES

Pack cucumbers in jars. While packing add one head and some stalk of dill, 1 clove of garlic, and a piece of yellow pepper, if desired. In the top of each jar, put a scant 1/4 tsp. powdered alum.

Measure and mix 3 cups water, 1 cup vinegar, and 1/4 cup salt. Pour over cucumbers hot and seal. (Makes enough liquid for two bottles).

I think one of my favorite aromas is the simmering of a pot of chili sauce on the stove. This is my favorite. Give it a try! My husband's favorite breakfast is sausage, hash browns, and eggs served with homemade chili sauce.

CHILI SAUCE

Peel and chop:
1 gallon tomatoes
1/2 cup onions

Boil for two hours with:
1/2 cup chopped green peppers
1/2 cup chopped red peppers
5 tsp. salt
1/2 cup brown sugar
1/2 tsp. cayenne pepper
1 tsp. nutmeg
2 tsp. ginger
1 tsp. cinnamon
1 tsp. mustard

Add:
1 quart vinegar and cook to desired consistency.
Pour into jars and seal.

Pickled beets are another family favorite and are easy to do.

PICKLED BEETS

Select small, young beets, cook until tender, dip into cold water, and peel off skins.

Mix together:
2 cups sugar
2 cups water
2 cups vinegar
1 tsp. allspice
1 lemon (thinly sliced)
1 T. cinnamon
1 tsp. cloves

Pour mixture over beets and simmer for 15 minutes. Pack into jars and seal.

Also, if you have finished a jar of sweet pickles, save the juice, open and drain a can of ordinary beets, and add them to the pickle juice. Let them stand in the refrigerator for a couple of days, and Presto! - more pickled beets with no waste.

Another fun addition to your canned goods shelf is this "Green Tomato Mincemeat". It is absolutely delicious in pies and it uses up the "last of the garden" crops.

DONNA'S GREEN TOMATO MINCEMEAT

Sprinkle 5 qts. ground green tomatoes with 1/4 cup salt, let stand overnight and drain. Add sufficient (3 cups) water to prevent sticking and cook for 30 minutes, stirring often.

Add:
1-1/4 cups lemon juice
Grated rind of one lemon
White of two lemons

Then add:
1 lb. seedless raisins
2 qts. ground apples (about 20)
1 lb. ground suet
2-1/2 lbs. brown sugar
1 tsp. cinnamon
1 tsp. nutmeg
1 tsp. cloves

Simmer for about 1 hour or until apples are tender and flavors are blended. Put in jars and seal. (5-6 qts.)

I think jams and jellies are one of the most rewarding things to can. I really recommend using a pectin since this is a big time saver, and you don't have to boil away so much fruit and juice. There are many brands, and I prefer Sure-Jel - just follow the directions, and you can't fail. The frozen type jams done with Sure-Jel are so fast and easy to do and are just like fresh fruit on your toast. (It's awfully good in the danish rolls, too!) We like the jams a little better than the jellies because we can utilize the fruits as well.

Canning is one way of preserving foods. Freezing is another. Nothing could be simpler than the process of freezing our produce. Many things can just be washed and frozen, such as blueberries. I always lay my berries on cookie sheets and freeze them and then put them in the plastic bags when they are frozen. This eliminates the problem of their freezing in one big chunk, and you can take out what you desire. This is a good idea with many things. Apple slices can be done like this, and then they are great for pies or apple pancakes. Rhubarb just needs to be washed and chopped in pieces and frozen. Don't forget to try my method for winter squash, mentioned in an earlier chapter.

Many times fresh coconuts are featured on special—try freezing these! Break them in half and shred or grate the meat, then freeze it in a bag. It's absolutely delicious and requires no sweetener, either!

Vegetables should be blanched before freezing. This stops the growing process and prevents aging of the vegetable. It also destroys enzymes that make the finished product less desirable.

Try doing sweet potatoes by the method I gave for squash and pumpkins. So easy!

Cook all your frozen vegetables directly from the freezer, especially corn on the cob. Cook it quickly in boiling water with a smidgen of sugar, and it will taste just like fresh corn and not "cobby", as some folks complain about frozen corn.

One thing I don't like my freezer to be without are small bags of chopped green pepper, parsley, chives, and other herbs. These sure do come in handy.

The other method we use in storing our produce is drying. This, too, can be done without all the expensive equipment we are often urged to buy. The first principle to remember in drying is that vegetables need to be blanched first, fruits do not. I simply use brown paper grocery sacks for drying because they are absorbent. Just slice your fruit, such as apples, or chop the blanched vegetables, then place them on your sacks so they are not touching and lay them in a warm dry place. By the furnace or water heater is good. If your climate is very dry, of course, outside in the sun is fine. It's a good idea to lay a cheesecloth or something similar over them to keep them clean. Where the climate is humid, I like to use the inside of my car, parked in the sun. Believe me, it gets warm in there! You also can dry things in your oven if you can set the temperature as low as 140°. Place the sacks in the oven and prop the door open slightly with a hot pad so the moisture can escape. It usually takes about 10-12 hours, depending on what you are drying and how small the pieces are. A rule of thumb to remember is that fruits should feel rubbery and pliable, and vegetables should be hard or crisp.

Some of my favorites to dry are:

Apple slices (Delicious apples work best)

Banana slices

Peach slices

Rhubarb pieces (great nibbling snack while hiking—they curb your thirst.)

Zucchini squash

Summer squash

Cucumber chips

Corn

All of these dried slices are great with a dip instead of those greasy potato chips.

And, of course, the fruit leathers. These can be done so simply and are really a favorite treat with the kids. Put a few pieces of fresh fruit in your blender (you can also use that last peach half in the bottle or any leftover canned fruit), then spread them on a cookie sheet that has been covered with plastic wrap. Spread the fruit quite thinly (about 1/4 inch) and dry it in your oven or by the other methods. Then, when dry, roll it up carefully in a roll, peeling off the plastic wrap. This can then be wrapped in plastic and frozen or sealed in glass jars in the oven using the method we discussed in Chapter 8 for the dried grains. However, when processing the leather in jars, use a temperature of only 165° rather than 225° as before. Another easy method that I like to use is to store some in a clean, old pillow case, hung in a cool, dark, dry place. It's so delicious, it's hard to keep around too long!

Drying things is one of the most exciting ways you can experiment with preserving foods. Be brave and try it!

Chapter X

Festive Fun Days on Frugal Funds

Even though we are all pinching our pennies and being practical, holidays and special days do roll around. The secret is to make them a fun, family affair without straining the budget. Let's go through the year and talk about some fun things we can do for each event.

New Year's Day starts us off. In the south, it's a custom to eat black-eyed peas on the first day of the new year for good luck in the coming year. This type of tradition can give us many pleasant memories with our family. It may be a new experience for many. Give them a try!

Valentine's Day is one of my favorites. I guess I am a sentimentalist at heart. This is a day to fix the special favorites of the one you love, to be served with lots of smiles and kisses! Be sure you include one red dish in your meal in the way of Jello salad, dessert, or pudding.

For Washington's Birthday, don't miss the opportunity to bake a cherry pie and tell the traditional story to your family. This can be done with great drama and excitement.

Everyone enjoys St. Patrick's Day even though we are of German, Danish, and English descent. We always have a dinner including something Irish and, of course, something green. Corned beef and cabbage was the only dish that didn't go over too well. I guess that my little "Germans" prefer their cabbage as Sauerkraut!

April Fool's Day is a great day for the Nitty Gritty Dinner. This is my daughter Kristen's favorite, and one the children really enjoy. The family are seated at the table with only a centerpiece and napkins, and are given a menu as follows for a four-course meal with three items for each course:

NITTY GRITTY DINNER	
Crane	(Fork)
Meaningful Measure	(Spoon)
Mint Stick	(Knife)
Floating Pine	(Glass of water with floating toothpick)
Pure Pilgrim	(Glass of milk)
Merry Mixers	(Relish plate)
Towering Inferno	(Hamburger patty with all the trimmings-cheese, tomato onion, using two lettuce leaves as the "bun" and placing a lighted birthday candle on top)
Manna	(Bread or bun)
Calorie Calamity	(Baked potato with butter and sour cream)
Hawaiian Rabbit	(Carrot and pineapple jello)
Tender Rounds	(Green Peas)
Hot and Cold	(Hot fudge sundae)

Of course, their menu lists only the imaginary dishes on the left-hand side. They each order their total meal at once from their menu, are served the first three things, then the table is cleared again, and they get the next three. It gets pretty funny since no one knows what he is getting. It can be a lot of fun. It's also a fun idea to make up your own menu.

For Easter, it is fun to save your old green plastic strawberry cartons and fill them with a little "Easter" grass and candy strawberries. These are delicious and so fun to eat. Not nearly as sweet as most candies. Tied up with plastic wrap and a red or green bow, they are always a hit with a shut-in or someone living all alone.

STRAWBERRIES

Mix together:
1 cup ground nuts
1 7-oz. package coconut
2 boxes strawberry jello
1 can sweetened condensed milk

Form like berries, dipping top in green sugar and rolling the rest of "berry" in red sugar.

Soak slivered almonds in a small amount of green coloring and water. Stick one almond sliver in top of each berry for the stem.

Speaking of Easter, that is one holiday that everyone gets in on. We always have the traditional family gathering where we all color boiled eggs. Each person tries to come up with the most clever bunch, and we really have an art show. The eggs are all placed in a basket and refrigerated to be enjoyed later.

A favorite Easter candy recipe is:

PEANUT BUTTER EGGS

Mix well:
1-1/2 boxes powdered sugar
1-1/2 cups peanut butter
2 sticks margarine (softened)
1-1/2 tsp. vanilla

Form into egg shapes and dip in chocolate.

None of our children care much for the sweet, commercial Easter egg candies, so we always have a treasure hunt, with each of them finding a nest at the end. The nest may contain anything from a novel they've been wanting, a record, or maybe a game or puzzle. This has been such a tradition in our family that even our 21-year-old son still enjoys his treasure hunt on Easter.

Spring is always the time for lots of weddings. Our basic mint recipe is so easy and versatile, you'll want to try it for all occasions.

BASIC MINTS

Knead together with hands:
8 oz. pkg. cream cheese
2 lb. pkg. powdered sugar

Color and flavor as desired:
Lemon - yellow
Mint - pink
Wintergreen - green

Mix colorings and flavoring in well.

Shape as desired.

For shower ideas or for a wedding, it's fun to make fragrant rice favors for each person. These are fun to use as a centerpiece in a small umbrella or just to hand out to guests.

FRAGRANT WEDDING RICE

Color desired amount of rice by placing it in a bowl of cold water and food coloring. Allow it to soak until it reaches the color you wish. Spread on cookie sheets and dry in a 200° oven until completely dry.

Then spray with favorite cologne and tie small amounts in squares of nylon net in compatible colors. Tie at the top with ribbons.

Later these favors are taken to the wedding, and the rice is thrown at the bride and groom.

The pièce de résistance is the French pastries. I learned to make these at a Relief Society Conference several years ago, and they have been a "hit" for me many times since.

FRENCH PASTRY

Bake one recipe cake (chocolate or yellow preferably) in a 11-1/2 x 17 x 1 inch cookie sheet. If using a cake mix, add one extra egg for a nicer texture. When cool, cut into small irregular shapes or triangles and freeze in pan.

When frozen, cut each small piece in half horizontally and fill with the following filling.

Filling

Drain juice from one 13-1/2 oz. can crushed pineapple into saucepan, saving crushed pineapple.

Bring to boil:
Pineapple juice
1/2 cup water
1/2 cup sugar

Dissolve 2 T. cornstarch in 2 T. water. Stir into boiling mixture, continue to stir until thickened.

Remove from heat and add:

4 T. lemon juice
Grated rind of one lemon (large)
Crushed pineapple

Stir until well blended.

Cherry pie filling may also be used, and is very good with the chocolate cake variety.

After pieces are filled, return to freezer. When completely frozen, frost sides only with the following icings:

Icing

Blend together:
1 lb. powdered sugar
1/3 cup shortening
1/3 cup milk
1/2 tsp. vanilla
Dash of salt
4 T. cocoa

Dip sides in chopped nuts, coconut, chocolate shot, or other decorating material.

From a decorator tube, squeeze icing gently back and forth on top of cake, until covered. Decorate with half a nut, cherry, decorator flowers.

Freeze uncovered. When firm, slide into plastic bags.

Don't pass by May 1st without having a May Basket of some sort. When the kids were small, we always made May Baskets from construction paper and filled them with popcorn, candies, and fresh spring flowers. They then delivered them to the homes of shut-ins and other friends. Traditionally, you are supposed to hang the basket on the door, knock, and run. If you're caught, they get a kiss!

When the kids got older, we baked a May Basket Cake for someone. You can either make a square cake and run a strip of cardboard over it, for the handle, and cover it with frosting; or bake your cake in a mixing bowl, invert it, and cover it with gumdrop roses. This is easy and Oh! so pretty.

To make gumdrop roses, roll a large gumdrop very thin on a sugar-covered board, cut the edges in three pieces for the petals, leaving a small triangle in the center. On a toothpick, roll each edge piece, one at a time, loosely forming the petals of a rose. Squeeze the bottom tightly to secure the petal to the toothpick and let harden. Leaves may be cut out of green gumdrops rolled very thinly. They may be cut in any shape. To form a curved leaf, lay over a pencil and allow to dry or harden. The large size gumdrops work best for rolling. Just be sure they are rolled almost transparently thin. Be inventive and see what type flowers you may create.

For birthdays at our house, the "birthday person" gets to choose the menu and at mealtime wears a silly little hat like the ones you see on New Year's Eve. The children get such a kick out of this family tradition. And when the birthday guest is a friend of the family, it makes that person feel really special, too. The meal would not be complete without our favorite "German Birthday Torte". This is a heavier-type cake that is to be refrigerated. Gosh! is it good!

GERMAN BIRTHDAY TORTE

Cream together:
1 stick margarine
1-1/2 cups sugar

Add and beat well:
3 eggs

Then add:
1/3 cup melted chocolate chips

Add:
1-1/4 cup milk, soured with 2 T. lemon juice

Then add:
2 cups flour
1 tsp. soda
1 tsp. salt

Pour into layer pans and sprinkle with the following mixture:

Mix together:
1/2 cup coconut
2/3 cup chocolate chips
3/4 cups graham cracker crumbs
1/2 cup nuts (chopped)
1/3 cup melted margarine

Bake at 375° for 35 minutes in layer pans.

Whip 1 cup whipping cream. Spread between and around sides of layers.

In the fall, nothing makes a party or special occasion more exciting than hot spiced cider and scones. The recipe for scones is in an earlier chapter.

GEORGEANNA'S HOT MULLED CIDER

In saucepan over low heat dissolve 1/4 cup light brown sugar, firmly packed, in 1 qt. cider or apple juice.

Add:
1/2 tsp. grated orange peel
1/4 cup orange juice
1/4 tsp. whole cloves
2 whole allspice
3 inch cinnamon stick
1 T. lemon juice
Dash of nutmeg

Bring to boil, reduce heat, and simmer uncovered for 20 minutes. Strain and discard spices.

Serve hot in punch cups with a cinnamon stick to use for stirring!

This is so good on a crisp fall evening with a bowl of shiny red apples.

For caramel corn that is absolutely "the best", try this one:

CARAMEL CORN

After discarding the unpopped or burned kernels, keep 6 qts. popped corn warm in a very slow oven while making the syrup.

Syrup

Melt:
2 sticks margarine

Stir in:
2 cups brown sugar (firmly packed)
1/2 cup corn syrup
1 tsp. salt

Bring to boil, stirring constantly.

Remove from heat and add:

1/2 tsp. soda
1 tsp. vanilla

Gradually pour over popped corn in a large bowl, mixing well with a fork. Turn into two large shallow baking pans. Bake at 250° for one hour, stirring every 15 minutes. Set pans out of oven; cool completely. Break caramelized corn apart.

Another good treat is this favorite caramel. If you like carameled apples, it's great for dipping the apples. They're Heidi's favorite. These caramels are so delicious and, yet, easy to make.

CARAMELS

Mix together in large pan:
2 cups sugar
1 large can Evaporated milk
1 cup dark Karo syrup
2 sticks margarine

Bring to boil, stirring constantly, and let boil for about 20 minutes. Add chopped nuts and 2 T. paraffin shavings. Pour into buttered 9x9 inch pan.

Christmas is the holiday of the year. There are so many ideas and recipes for this holiday I'd like to share with you, I hardly know where to start. The first thing we make at our house are gingerbread houses. There is always one with our address on, and then we make several to give to our friends. If you do these in mass production, they go fast and are less expensive to make. It's surprising how many new ideas we keep coming up with to decorate them. The aroma of a gingerbread house really sets the mood for Christmas. Every Christmas, a theme is selected at our home to follow for Christmas. I think our favorite was a complete gingerbread theme. We hung gingerbread boys and girls in the windows, outlined our front door in ruffled nylon net, twinkly lights, and little gingerbread people, and our tree was covered with twinkly lights, gingerbread cookies, and calico bows. We wrapped all our packages in brown wrapping paper and used calico scraps cut with pinking shears as bows and ribbons. It was so special! and inexpensive! One year our theme was poinsettias. We made them out of red burlap, spray starched, and tied in yellow yarn pom-pom centers. We tied the flowers all over the tree and used them all over the house in our decorating. It was very effective.

Another tradition we always carry out is our Wishbone Basket. All through the year we save the wishbones from our chickens and turkeys. Then, at Christmas time, they are rubbed well with sandpaper, and Roy paints them white. These are kept in a little basket, each tied with red yarn. As friends and neighbors visit our home over the holidays, they are invited to write their family name on a wishbone, make a wish, and tie it on our tree. As we trim our tree each year, it's so much fun to see the names of dear friends from the many places we have lived.

There is a certain list of family favorites that are prepared every Christmas. If one recipe is left out, someone is disappointed. We usually start preparing them right after Thanksgiving, because nearly all can be frozen and keep well. The Sunday before Christmas, we assemble several baskets of these goodies, taking them to homes of special people. We always leave them at their door with a carol or two.

CHEWY GINGER COOKIES

Mix well:
1 stick margarine
1/4 cup solid shortening
1 cup packed brown sugar
1 egg
1/4 cup molasses

Add:
2-1/4 cups flour
2 tsp. soda
1/4 tsp. salt
1 tsp. ginger
1 tsp. cinnamon
1/2 tsp. cloves

Chill, roll in balls, dip top side in sugar, and sprinkle with 2-3 drops of water. Set balls on cookie sheet and bake at 375° for 10-12 minutes.

ROCKY ROAD

In saucepan, combine:
1 cup semi-sweet chocolate morsels
1 cup butterscotch morsels
1/2 cup peanut butter

Place over very low heat and melt until mixture is blended and smooth.

Add:
3 cups miniature marshmallows
1 cup salted peanuts

Mix well. Spread in a foil-lined 8 inch square pan. Chill until firm.

OATMEAL FUDGE

Mix together:
2 cups sugar
1/2 cup milk
1 stick margarine
3 T. cocoa
1/2 tsp. salt

Bring to boil slowly. Boil for one minute.

Add:
3 cups quick oats
1/2 cup nuts (chopped)
1 cup coconut
1 tsp. vanilla

Remove from heat quickly and stir until thick. Drop by spoonfuls onto wax paper. Let harden.

CHOCOLATE RAISIN CLUSTERS

Melt 2 pkgs. (12 oz.) semi-sweet chocolate morsels.

Blend in one 15 oz. can sweetened condensed milk.

Remove from heat and stir in:
2 tsp. vanilla
1/4 tsp. salt
2 cups raisins

Drop by spoonfuls onto wax paper. Let harden and chill.

Some of the other goodies we always make are included in other parts of the book, such as caramels (at Christmas, we dip them in chocolate or make turtles by dropping a spoonful of caramel on 4 pecan halves and "frosting" them with melted chocolate), nutbreads (which I bake in little juice cans, wrap them in foil or plastic wrap, with a small construction paper flame on top to resemble candles), the sweet rolls (which we form as Swedish tea-rings and decorate with frosting, pecans, and maraschino cherries), and our mints. We mix up the "Basic Mints" dough, leaving out the mint, and then we use it as a base for all our centers to dip in chocolate. You can add as much coconut as you can mix in, then roll in balls and dip in chocolate, or mix in cherries, nuts, a little almond extract, and pink coloring, or use maple extract and nuts, or orange or lemon flavoring and peel, or whatever you like. It's also good to add 3-4 tablespoonfuls or more of cocoa and a pat of real butter to the basic dough, knead it well, add chopped nuts, form in balls, and roll in chocolate shot. I even like to add a dash of mint because I like the choco-mint combination. These are especially pretty and refreshing to serve after a HOT Mexican dinner. (The "Strawberry" recipe I gave you earlier in this chapter makes a colorful addition to a box of homemade candies, as well as the "Basic Mints".)

All of our homemade goodies, along with lots of fruits and nuts, keep the nibblers happy during Christmas time at the Nye's. All of our traditions, as well as the spiritual overtone in our activities, make the gifts take a backseat to the holiday, which we feel is the way it should be. It is certainly the time of the year that love burns warm, and our relationship with our Father in Heaven is very special in our hearts.

A tradition that I am starting with my children, as they marry and start their own homes, is to buy a one place setting of a very bright, cheery, special pattern of china. My children then reserve this one setting for special occasions—for that person who is having a birthday, got a raise, a perfect report card, or just needed the family to say we love you and you're extra special to us today.

I hope my children will always remember how important the little things in life are and how much they can mean to those around them. May you, too, have happy special occasions, holidays, or just special moments with the loved ones in your home.

Chapter XI

Who Can Find a Virtuous Woman?

It's been a real delight visiting with you in my kitchen. I hope some of the ideas, suggestions, and recipes will be as fun for you and your family as they have been for mine. Before we part, I would like to share a few other ideas on homemaking outside the kitchen.

First of all, to be a happy, cheerful homemaker you must be a happy, cheerful person. I strongly feel we must like ourselves and be pleased with ourselves before we can be pleasant to others. Remember, Christ said to "love thy neighbor as *thyself*". Nearly always when we find ourselves yelling at the children or upset with our husbands, it is really because we are unhappy with ourselves.

Be good to yourself. Take care of yourself and think of yourself as a person. Too often we become martyrs and then we not only make ourselves unhappy and bone weary, but we upset our whole family, too. To be a martyr merely makes our husbands and children feel guilty and uncomfortable, when they really don't expect as much of us as we do of ourselves. Many times my husband has told me that he is much happier when I am rested and "prettied up" when he comes home than when I have worked like a slave and am miserable.

Wives, again I say, be good to yourselves. Take a short rest each day, take time to keep yourself looking pleasant and attractive, and take time to grow by reading the scriptures and learning new things. The whole family will follow your lead and be uplifted.

Attitude is so important. If you think of yourself as "somebody", everyone else will, too. If we think positive thoughts, we can't fail. Try playing "Pollyanna" and look for the good in everything. It really is amazing how it catches on and spreads, first to your family, and then to everyone you come in contact with. Your enthusiasm makes you feel so much better inside, and you'll be a lot more pleasant to be with on the outside. This is one very important principle we have tried to instill in the lives of our children. It has paid off in so many ways, such as in faith, accomplishments, and happy smiles. It's such a good feeling, thinking pleasant thoughts!

Much has been said about being good mothers, and I feel that there is endless material to help us in this phase of our lives. However, as my friends will testify, I am a firm believer in the fact that we are wives first! Only through success as wives can we become total successes as mothers.

Work hard at being good wives! Give it all you've got! The benefits are tremendous. Husbands can be such fun. There is nothing a husband won't do for a wife, if he knows she is giving him her all. It is so rewarding to do nice little things for him, and just showing him love and understanding does great things for your morale. A husband also appreciates us looking nice because it reflects on his abilities in life. He likes to be proud of us.

Little notes tucked in a lunch box or the pocket of his overcoat can bring a warm feeling in his heart all day. I like to mail a funny card or note to Roy's office occasionally, so that as he opens the morning mail, he knows that I appreciate his working to provide me with things. Candlelight dinners after the children are in bed have been very meaningful in our closeness. Walks together are another experience we enjoy, and it gives us a special time to communicate. Two things my mother taught me about being a good wife were to freshen up my appearance right before my husband arrives home in the evening and to always have the table set for dinner. Then, even if the food isn't completely prepared, he has the feeling that dinner is underway, and this is pleasing to him. I have tried to practice these things almost as a ritual, and it works! Try it!

Women, if you are too busy or too tired to be good wives, your priorities are in the wrong order. Re-evaluate your life and schedule, and see how happy everyone (including yourself) in your family becomes.

Roy has often quoted to me or written on a note the choice scripture in Proverbs 31:10-31 :

"Who can find a virtuous woman? for her price is far above rubies.

The heart of her husband doth safely trust in her, so that he shall have no need of spoil.

She will do him good and not evil all the days of her life.

She seeketh wool, and flax, and worketh willingly with her hands.

She is like the merchants' ships; she bringeth her food from afar.

She riseth also while it is yet night, and giveth meat to her household, and a portion to her maidens.

She considereth a field, and buyeth it: with the fruit of her hands she planteth a vineyard.

She girdeth her loins with strength, and strengtheneth her arms.

She perceiveth that her merchandise is good: her candle goeth not out by night.

She layeth her hands to the spindle, and her hands hold the distaff.

She stretcheth out her hand to the poor; yea, she reacheth forth her hands to the needy.

She is not afraid of the snow for her household: for all her household are clothed with scarlet.

She maketh herself coverings of tapestry; her clothing is silk and purple.

Her husband is known in the gates, when he sitteth among the elders of the land.

She maketh fine linen, and selleth it; and delivereth girdles unto the merchant.

Strength and honour are her clothing; and she shall rejoice in time to come.

She openeth her mouth with wisdom; and in her tongue is the law of kindness.

She looketh well to the ways of her household, and eateth not the bread of idleness.

Her children arise up, and call her blessed; her husband also, and he praiseth her.

Many daughters have done virtuously, but thou excellest them all.

Favour is deceitful, and beauty is vain: but a woman that feareth the Lord, she shall be praised.

Give her of the fruit of her hands; and let her own works praise her in the gates.

I really feel blessed that the little things I can do for him pay off in such love as this.

We wear many hats in our roles as wives and mothers, but we always must keep foremost in our minds priorities and moderation in all things. Keep a tidy house but enjoy it. It should be "clean enough to look nice but dirty enough to be comfortable". Love your children and discipline them, but enjoy them and play with them, too. We have always tried to stress the specialness of homemaking skills so the children wanted to help, and that's how they learned the skills. By spending time with them and helping with their activities, we in turn were helped. Through this understanding and togetherness, we have been able to participate in and enjoy many things that wouldn't have been possible on our budget or time schedule. Many happy hours and learning experiences were enjoyed as we all worked together on the home bakery routes we had in Kansas City and Dallas. Nor will any of us forget the special times working in our large garden or remodeling one of our houses.

A bit of psychology I have always used with my family is to always expect them to do the right thing or their best. If you assume that, they will never let you down. I guess it's that old "positive thinking" again. Another thing I try to do is to compliment my children or husband to someone else when they are within earshot. It's surprising how motivating this can be. My family seem to be much more pleased if they think I'm telling someone else when I don't know they can hear than if I compliment them on their own.

Family pride and spirit can be a tremendous thing—compare this to a community. I'm sure we've all lived in communities where the spirit, enthusiasm, and closeness were exciting and contagious. Then there are others where every home seems a separate island. Everyone knows which is the most rewarding. Let's all strive for family pride. Start when the children are tiny. Be proud of your name and what you stand for. Every time our children leave home, Roy admonishes them to "Remember who you are". We are all children of God and should be striving to have our "Heaven on Earth" within our homes.

Brother Leslie Stone once said, "Mothers hold in their hands the destiny of nations." Think about that one—it's so true. What we are all comes from the home. It can be so rewarding to teach our children the things they should know. ·Remember our talking about manners and table etiquette in Chapter 1?

Another opportunity I used as a learning time for the kids was when they were pre-schoolers but didn't require a nap in the afternoon any longer. I still felt it was vital that they rest awhile and at least slow down from their busy activities. So after a half hour rest, we would have learning or school time. They all looked forward to this time with eagerness. One day we would learn about colors, one day about the seasons, and I remember one day we had so much fun learning how to use the telephone properly. We all had many laughs that day. We also spent times learning a little fire drill for the home, our names and addresses fully, and many more helpful things. This gave me an opportunity to rest from my work, and we all benefited from the time together. Some days we would take a walk or lie on the bed and tell make-believe stories—what a delightful experience! It reminds me of what Marion D. Hanks once said, "Our callings are not weights but wings."

One particular rainy day, we were enjoying the story of *Bambi*, in which Thumper says, "If you can't say something nice, don't say anything at all." This really made an impression as we discussed it, and we still remind one another of this in our home today!

If there is one rule to go by in raising children, I feel it is to be consistent. You can accomplish anything, and your children will feel so much more secure. It can be hard at times, but Oh! so worthwhile. Keep that in the back of your mind always when dealing with your children. Through consistency, family rules and traditions will become established, and a happy home will blossom forth.

Thanks for stopping by. It's been a pleasant time for me, and I hope for you, also.

Smile always!

Index

About the Author

Beverly K. Nye was raised on a farm in Nebraska and still has vivid memories of her family making good use of the abundance of home grown fruits, vegetables and grains in season and canning and preserving them for out-of-season use. This, coupled with her Mormon upbringing, has provided much of the basis for this book.

Practicing creativity, economy and good old-fashioned nutrition, she has raised a family of four children while living in ten different locations in the United States. Frequent moving has given her an appreciation of various ways of life and has contributed to the wide assortment of recipes she has collected over the years. She has taught home economics for over 20 years in homemaking classes and appears frequently on television midday talk shows.

Mrs. Nye has, for years, practiced the Mormon teaching of having a year's supply of necessary food and other staples on hand. She feels when you no longer must buy and are versed in the art of food storage, you can be a truly discriminating shopper, taking the best possible advantage of bargains. She also practices her belief that the family is the key to the good life.